PRESENTED TO:

_____

FROM:

_____

DATE:

_____

OTHER BOOKS BY ANNE GRAHAM LOTZ

The Vision of His Glory

God's Story

Daily Light

Just Give Me Jesus

Heaven: My Father's House

My Heart's Cry

Why? Trusting God When You Don't Understand

The Joy of My Heart

My Jesus Is ... Everything

I Saw the Lord

The Magnificent Obsession

Heaven: God's Promise for Me

Expecting to See Jesus

Wounded by God's People

The Daniel Prayer

The Daniel Key

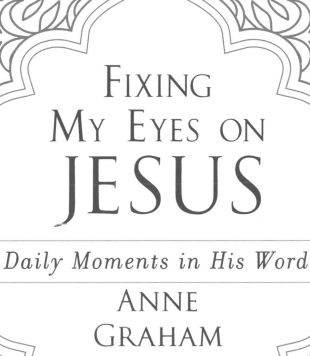

Fixing My Eyes on JESUS

Daily Moments in His Word

ANNE GRAHAM LOTZ

365
DEVOTIONS

ZONDERVAN
.com

INTRODUCTION

Having grown up in the mountains of western North Carolina, I have always enjoyed hiking. One fourteen-mile hike I took as a young teen stands out particularly in my mind because somewhere along the way, my companion and I got completely lost in a huge laurel thicket!

When we realized we were lost, my friend took a compass out of his pocket, noted the needle pointing north, and as a result adjusted our direction. We chose the right way out and eventually emerged where we needed to be.

Getting up early in the morning to fix my eyes on Jesus through prayer and reading His Word is like setting my spiritual compass each day. No matter what faces me during the day, or how "lost" and confused I may become, no matter how many decisions and choices I'm confronted with, my heart and my thoughts always turn toward Him. And He invariably leads me on the right path.

My prayer is that the devotions in this small volume will help you fix your eyes on Jesus every day so that you, too, can set your spiritual compass, ensuring that you center on Him and stay on the right path.

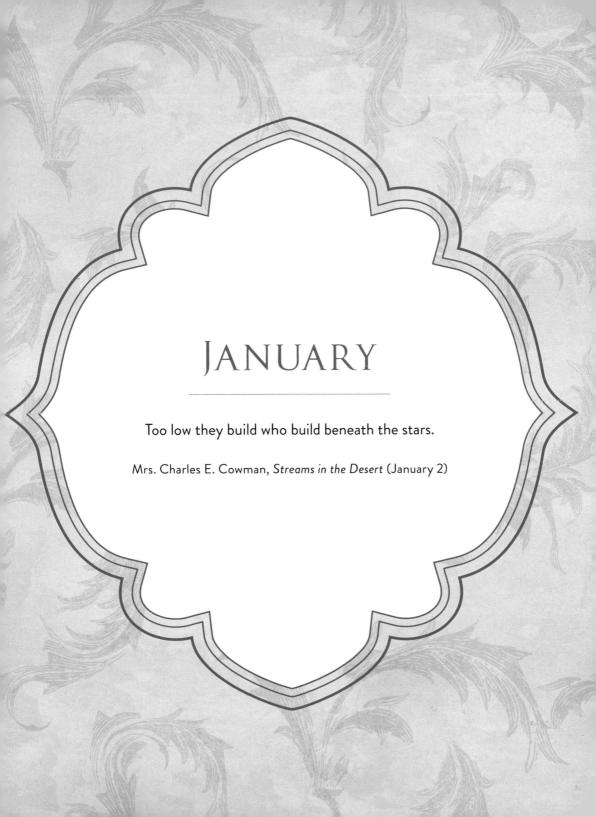

JANUARY

Too low they build who build beneath the stars.

Mrs. Charles E. Cowman, *Streams in the Desert* (January 2)

THE GOD OF THE SECOND CHANCE

Forgetting what is behind and straining toward what is
ahead, I press on toward the goal to win the prize for
which God has called me heavenward in Christ Jesus.
Philippians 3:13–14

I once heard a speaker ask what we thought God expected of us. Mentally I answered, *Righteousness, holiness, love for God and my neighbor.*

He repeated his question, so I continued my list: *Bible reading, prayer, obedience, service.*

But then he stated, to my stunned amazement, "All God ever expects of you is failure."

I had to resist the temptation to raise my hand, wave it wildly, and exclaim, "I can do that! I can live up to God's expectations! I know I can fail!"

But before I could blurt it out, the speaker said, "But He has given you the Holy Spirit so that you need never fail."

As we begin the new year, have you stopped making resolutions because of repeated failure to keep the old ones? Do your past failures discourage you in the present and paralyze you for the future? Then join me in praising the God who expects us in our flesh to fail, but who is also the God of the second chance!

He Will Restore You

> Do you not know? Have you not heard? The LORD
> is the everlasting God, the Creator of the ends of
> the earth. He will not grow tired or weary, and his
> understanding no one can fathom. He gives strength
> to the weary and increases the power of the weak.
> *Isaiah 40:28–29*

John 6:3 says, "Jesus went up on a mountainside and sat down with his disciples." I imagine they were surrounded by green grass dotted with wildflowers, the snowcapped Mount Hermon in the background, and the blue Sea of Galilee in the foreground. Their weary spirits must have felt like men coming off a sun-scorched desert, looking for water!

As Jesus and His disciples rested on the mountainside, we have the beautiful picture of the Good Shepherd making His sheep lie down in green pastures, leading them beside still waters.

Just as He knew the demands that would be made on the disciples, Jesus also knows the demands on your life. And He will provide a way for you to meet those demands. Jesus wants you to sit down with Him!

Spend time alone with Him today in the green pasture of His Word. He will restore you—on the inside!

HE IS WITH YOU

"And surely I am with you always, to
the very end of the age."
Matthew 28:20

When you ask, "God, where are You?" or, "Why did You let this happen?" or say, "I just don't understand," are you overlooking the fact that Jesus has drawn near to you?

God promises in Isaiah 43:2, "When you pass through the waters, I will be with you." Is it possible you are blinded to His presence by your own tears? Are you deafened to His gentle voice by your own accusations?

God doesn't always protect those He loves from suffering or answer our prayers the way we ask Him to, but He does promise in His Word that He will be present with us in the midst of our suffering and pain. And that when we pass through the waters, He will be with us, and when we pass through the rivers, they will not sweep over us (Isaiah 43:2).

He is the Lord, your God, your Savior. You are precious and honored in His sight. He is saying to you, "I'm here!"

THE RIGHT WAY

For the LORD watches over the way of the righteous,
but the way of the wicked will perish.
Psalm 1:6

Sometimes as I think about the accomplishments of others, just for a moment I wonder, *What if …?* But then, almost immediately, I'm reminded that God has given me my own unique purpose in life.

Psalm 23:3 says, "He guides me in paths of righteousness for his name's sake." To find and follow those paths, to work out His purpose for our lives, will require reading and studying God's Word and praying about how it applies to us. It will involve obedience and service. Not because we have to but because we love Jesus. That's the path He has laid out before us.

With all your heart just follow Jesus. From personal experience, I can assure you, you'll be blessed. Satisfied. Fulfilled. He will never mislead you. He will lead you right. Follow Him!

FINISH HIS WORK

"I have brought you glory on earth by
completing the work you gave me to do."
John 17:4

You were created for the purpose of glorifying God through the Christlike character of your life and the effectiveness of your service. The Bible says, "You were bought at a price; therefore glorify God in your body and in your spirit, which are God's" (1 Corinthians 6:20–21 NKJV).

If you are able to finish God's work, it won't be an accident. It'll be because you have focused every minute of every day on God's purpose. And that purpose determines the way you manage your time, money, priorities, relationships, career, and every other aspect of your life. God isn't something you add to your life—He *is* your life! And your life's work.

To know God is to love God. To love Him is to serve Him. To serve Him is to know Him better. To know Him better is to love Him more. So start getting to know God, and then keep the cycle going until you've finished.

CLOSE TO THE BROKENHEARTED

The Spirit of the Sovereign LORD is on me, because the LORD
has anointed me to preach good news to the poor. He has
sent me to bind up the brokenhearted, to proclaim freedom
for the captives and release from darkness for the prisoners.

Isaiah 61:1

Perhaps the most powerful moment in our New Orleans *Just Give Me Jesus* arena revival occurred when Sheila Bailey stopped her prayer session to share the love and compassion of Jesus with a hurting woman. The woman had spontaneously come forward, in her brokenness and despair, to the front of the arena filled with thousands of women.

And in that Spirit-filled moment, Sheila reflected a loving Father who's never too busy or preoccupied to hear your cry, to wrap His arms of love around you, and to give you Fatherly counsel. Psalm 34:18 declares, "The LORD is close to the brokenhearted and saves those who are crushed in spirit."

Are you suffering today with troubles that threaten to overwhelm you? Then be assured. He loves you. Go to Him. He hears your cry. You're not an interruption. You're His child.

GOD REMEMBERS

For his anger lasts only a moment, but his favor
lasts a lifetime; weeping may remain for a night,
but rejoicing comes in the morning.
Psalm 30:5

God remembers! The Bible says in Genesis 8:1, "God remembered Noah and all … that were with him in the ark, and he sent a wind over the earth, and the waters receded." God remembered! Not because He had forgotten. It simply means the time had come for God to act on His own initiative.

It required nothing of Noah except patient waiting during all those days and weeks when the flood had covered the entire earth. Then, I wonder … did Noah one morning throw back the shutters of the ark and gasp as the brilliant sunshine stung his eyes? Did he shout his praise to the God who'd sent the storm—and now the wind to calm the seas and the sun to dry the earth?

Noah knew God remembered him.

And God remembers you! This may be the time for patient waiting. The time to long for the storm to be over. But the day is coming for the brilliant sun to shine after the storm. Because … God remembers!

LOOK UP!

Jesus rebuked the demon, and it came out of the
boy, and he was healed from that moment.
Matthew 17:18

One of the pictures in John Bunyan's *Pilgrim's Progress* is a man sorting through a can of garbage. He carefully takes out the little bits of tinsel he finds in the garbage can. Behind him is an angel who's offering him a solid gold crown studded with precious jewels. But the man is so engrossed in the garbage he never notices the angel.

When we get to heaven, will we be ashamed of our preoccupation with garbage in this life—garbage that prevented us from turning around, leaving it all behind, and reaching out for what God wanted to give us? First Corinthians 2:9 says, "No eye has seen, no ear has heard, no mind has conceived what God has prepared for those who love him."

So look up! Stop clinging so tightly to what you want. Don't lose out on what God wants to give you.

TRUST HIM

Trust in the LORD with all your heart and lean not on
your own understanding; in all your ways acknowledge
him, and he will make your paths straight.

Proverbs 3:5–6

We simply have to trust our heavenly Father to know best. We have to trust God's silences and wait for God's answers.

When we pray for the healing of a loved one, and he or she dies ... when we pray for release from a financial burden, and things just seem to get worse ... when we pray for reconciliation, and we're handed divorce papers ... when we pray for our career, and we get laid off ... when we pray for protection, and we're robbed ... *trust Him.*

Psalm 37:5 says, "Commit your way to the LORD, trust also in Him, and He shall bring it to pass" (NKJV). God answers prayer in His time and in His way—so that our faith rests totally in Him. Then, when the answer comes, we know without a shadow of doubt that it comes from Him alone.

So ... commit your way to Him and trust Him.

A Fresh Vision of Jesus

When I saw him, I fell at his feet as though dead.
Then he placed his right hand on me and said: "Do
not be afraid. I am the First and the Last."
Revelation 1:17

Like John on Patmos, are you cut off from family and friends?
Or flat on your back in a hospital?

Or trapped in a body that's filled with pain?

Or in a marriage where the love has run out?

When John's need for Jesus was overwhelming, he looked up and received a fresh vision of Jesus. If John hadn't been exiled on the island of Patmos for his faith, I wonder if we'd have the last book in our Bible. As a book that has brought hope to generations because it relates John's vision of Jesus, it tells us the end of God's story . . . and it's Jesus!

Are you on Patmos? Use your situation as an opportunity to look up. Then re-surrender to the lordship of Jesus!

MORE THAN JUST ENOUGH

Brothers, I do not consider myself yet to have taken
hold of it. But one thing I do: Forgetting what is
behind and straining toward what is ahead, I press
on toward the goal to win the prize for which God
has called me heavenward in Christ Jesus.

Philippians 3:13–14

What's the desire of your heart? Are you satisfied with just enough, or do you want more? More peace, more hope, more joy, more love, more fulfillment?

I want more! I want more than just being saved from God's wrath, more than calling myself a Christian, more than just a ticket to heaven, more than the bare minimum God offers.

I've concluded that it won't be enough until, like the apostle Paul, my faith becomes sight and I know Him as fully as I am known by Him (see 1 Corinthians 13:12). I long for everything God wants to give me. I want more of His image reflected in my life. More of His Spirit in my service. More of His glory on my knees.

What are you longing for? If you want more, isn't it time you began embracing the God-filled life?

THE SHEPHERD'S VOICE

"I am the good shepherd; I know my
sheep and my sheep know me."
John 10:14

Does something about being a Christian confuse you? Some issues are so basic, so clear-cut and obvious, they are not confusing—such as that we're all sinners, separated from God; that God sent His Son to be our Savior; that those who receive Jesus Christ by faith are born again into the family of God.

But other issues, especially those related specifically to your life, are not as clear: whether or not you should marry, take a particular job, have surgery, sell your house. Those issues may involve your relationships, your home, your future. The list is endless, isn't it?

How do you and I know what to do? We follow the Lord, our Shepherd, who leads us beside "quiet waters" and guides us in the "paths of righteousness" (see Psalm 23). Sometimes we don't know what to do, which is why we follow the Shepherd. Because He does.

JESUS WEPT

Praise be to the God and Father of our Lord Jesus Christ! In
his great mercy he has given us new birth into a living hope
through the resurrection of Jesus Christ from the dead.

1 Peter 1:3

When have you thought, *Jesus just doesn't care,* or *If God really loved me, He would've prevented this circumstance I'm in?*

All these thoughts crowding your mind are like seeds sown by Satan. And if you're not alert, those seeds will grow into weeds that choke out and strangle the truth—that God loves you, that your grief is His and your pain is His . . . that your tears are on His face.

At the grave of Lazarus, "Jesus wept" (John 11:35). He wept for no other reason than that He loved Lazarus and his sisters, Martha and Mary, and this precious family was weeping. He was entering into their suffering even as one day He would ask us to enter into His.

When your spirit is heavy, when your heart is broken, when your burdens seem unbearable—trust Him. Look to Him. Your tears are on His face!

HIS REBUKE

Whoever touches you touches the apple of his eye.
Zechariah 2:8

When Mary poured out expensive perfume over Jesus' feet, it was with no concern for the cost. This was for Jesus. Nothing was too good for Him. But the moment was shattered when Judas asked, "Why wasn't this perfume sold and the money given to the poor?" (John 12:5).

In other words, "You're wasting your ointment on Him. Jesus is not worth it!" And remember: Judas was a disciple, one of Jesus' twelve closest friends.

Who has sneered at *your* love for Jesus? Who has said, "You're wasting your time, your gifts"? Who's made fun of your faith—for staying in your marriage? For refusing to lie and steal and cheat? For remaining sexually pure?

Was it another believer, a disciple? Then take note of how Jesus rebuked Judas: "Leave her alone," He said (John 12:7).

Those who sneer at you and make fun of you need to watch out or they will find themselves facing the stern rebuke of One who says, "Leave her alone."

A Tree ... or a Twig?

Blessed is the man who does not walk in the counsel of the
wicked or stand in the way of sinners or sit in the seat of
mockers. But his delight is in the law of the LORD, and on
his law he meditates day and night. He is like a tree planted
by streams of water, which yields its fruit in season and
whose leaf does not wither. Whatever he does prospers.

Psalm 1:1–3

God plants you and me in our faith to grow us into "trees" of right-eousness. He uses adversity to make us strong. And He leads us to endure—not "somehow," but victoriously as we choose to trust Him.

King David knew that the secret of victory over adversity was a conscious choice to trust God. He cried out in prayer, "How long must I wrestle with my thoughts and every day have sorrow in my heart?... But I trust in your unfailing love" (Psalm 13:2, 5). David exercised his will to trust God even when he didn't feel like it. He had learned to walk by faith, not by feelings.

What about you? Will you grow into a tree of righteousness—or remain a twig? Will you have victory over adversity—or remain defeated? It's your choice. Choose to be strong! Choose to trust in Him!

PRAISE HIM NOW!

> That which was from the beginning, which we have
> heard, which we have seen with our eyes, which we
> have looked at and our hands have touched —this
> we proclaim concerning the Word of life.
> *1 John 1:1*

What has Jesus done for you? What things that Jesus has done for you have your family, your friends, your neighbors, your coworkers, your teammates heard you describe?

The apostle John testified that "many people, because they had heard that [Jesus] had given this miraculous sign, went out to meet him" (John 12:18). Who is asking to meet Jesus because of what He has done for you? When have you told someone about how He forgave your sin and removed your guilt? When have you told someone about the prayer He answered, the disease He healed, or the promise He fulfilled?

Praise Him! When Jesus was told by the religious leaders to rebuke the people for praising Him, He said if they didn't, then even the rocks would cry out (see Luke 19:40).

Don't leave it to the rocks. Praise Him now!

CRUCIFIED ... TO LIVE!

"I tell you the truth, unless a kernel of wheat falls
to the ground and dies, it remains only a single
seed. But if it dies, it produces many seeds."
John 12:24

God wants to bless you even more than you could think to ask. But the fullness of His blessing comes only as you fully release your will, your goals, your ambitions, your desires, and your thoughts to Him.

The apostle Paul said, "I have been crucified with Christ and I no longer live, but Christ lives in me. The life I live in the body, I live by faith in the Son of God, who loved me and gave himself for me" (Galatians 2:20). Crucifixion is a slow, painful death to your *self* as God allows problems and pain into your life to act as the nails that pin you to the cross. These things are often a part of life anyway, but in the life of a child of God, they're not wasted.

Jesus calls us to deny ourselves, take up His cross, and follow Him. But never forget: after the cross come the resurrection and the glory and the crown.

YOU HAVE HIS PRESENCE

"When you pass through the waters, I will
be with you; and when you pass through the
rivers, they will not sweep over you."
Isaiah 43:2

The Bible says when adversity increases in intensity, you have God's presence. When others criticize you, you have God's presence. When you're overwhelmed by burdens or depression, you have God's presence. When you're isolated from those you love and cut off from people, you have God's presence.

Praise God that He lives within us, and He has promised, "Never will I leave you; never will I forsake you" (Hebrews 13:5). And He has assured us, "Surely I am with you always, to the very end of the age" (Matthew 28:20).

God may not deliver you from pain or pressure or problems. He may not prevent you from that disease or divorce or disaster. But He does promise to be with you wherever you go and in whatever situation you face. God is with you ... right here ... right now.

BE HUMBLE

He humbled you, causing you to hunger and then feeding
you with manna, which neither you nor your fathers had
known, to teach you that man does not live on bread alone
but on every word that comes from the mouth of the LORD.
Deuteronomy 8:3

Whose offer of help are you refusing out of pride? When Jesus approached Peter to wash his feet, Peter pulled back. He said, "Lord, are you going to wash my feet?"

Jesus replied, "You don't realize now what I am doing, but later you will understand."

As Jesus bent down to pour the water over Peter's grimy feet, Peter protested, "No, you'll never wash my feet" (see John 13:3–8).

Peter was unwilling to humble himself and allow Jesus to do something for him that he didn't understand. His attitude was so typical of you and me. It can be a serious wound to our pride to *be* served. Whose offer of help *are* you refusing for prideful reasons? Are you refusing to even admit you need any help at all?

God clearly commands us in Scripture to "humble yourselves" (see, for example, James 4:10; 1 Peter 5:6). Be obedient to His command. Express your obedience in a willingness to *be* served!

DON'T BE AFRAID

*After this, the word of the LORD came to
Abram in a vision: "Do not be afraid, Abram. I
am your shield, your very great reward."*
Genesis 15:1

Jesus said with quiet authority, "Do not let your hearts be troubled" (John 14:1). It's a command you and I are to obey. Deliberately calming ourselves is a choice we're to make in the face of setbacks, accidents, failures, and all kinds of other calamities that cause us to be terrified of the consequences.

In the midst of our fear, Jesus commands us to stop letting our imaginations run wild, to stop analyzing every detail again and again.

Peace begins with a choice to stop being afraid, followed by a decision to start trusting God. It's been said that peace is not the absence of danger but the presence of God. When I toss and turn in the middle of the night, worried over some troublesome situation in my life, I'm comforted and calmed as I meditate on who God is.

When you tend to be afraid … don't be. Trust *Him*!

CONSISTENCE IN DEPENDENCE

Pray continually.
1 Thessalonians 5:17

In what areas of your life are you acting *independently* of God? I can usually determine those areas in my life by just checking the things I haven't prayed about: the people and problems, the relationships, the attitudes, the decisions—anything and everything I haven't talked to Him about.

If my heart's cry is to be more fruitful for Him, then one of the goals of my life needs to be that I more consistently depend on Him. Jesus said, "I am the vine; you are the branches. If a man remains in me and I in him, he will bear much fruit; apart from me you can do nothing" (John 15:5).

So examine your prayer life. Make it your goal to be more consistent in depending on Him. Submit every part of your daily activities, your thoughts and will and emotions to Jesus in prayer. Then move forward—on your knees!

THE TRADE-OFF

For this reason, since the day we heard about you, we have
not stopped praying for you and asking God to fill you with
the knowledge of his will through all spiritual wisdom and
understanding. And we pray this in order that you may live
a life worthy of the Lord and may please him in every way.

Colossians 1:9–10

What sin is preventing the Holy Spirit from filling your life?
God's Word commands us to "be filled with the Spirit" (Ephesians 5:18). That means making sure you keep short accounts with the Lord where sin is concerned, every day confessing by name the sin you are conscious of having committed that day and asking God for cleansing so you will maintain sweet fellowship with Him.

Are you thinking, *That's too much trouble. Besides, the sin in my life is so small, it can't make that much difference,* or *I could never quit that. I enjoy it too much*? Whatever your excuse, is it worth the trade-off? Is it worth losing out on an intimate relationship with God as the price for clinging to your sin?

Jesus said, "Love the Lord your God with all your heart and with all your soul and with all your mind" (Matthew 22:37). Love Him more than you love your sin. That's a command!

THE AUTHENTIC VOICE

You must not listen to the words of that prophet or
dreamer. The LORD your God is testing you to find
out whether you love him with all your heart and
with all your soul. It is the LORD your God you must
follow, and him you must revere. Keep his commands
and obey him; serve him and hold fast to him.

Deuteronomy 13:3–4

A lot of people *claim* to speak for God! But are their voices authentic? Sometimes they say, "God told me to tell you if you had more faith, you'd be healed," or "If He loved you, you wouldn't have lost your job," or "If God really loved you, your spouse wouldn't have walked out."

Such words by sincere people can put us into a tailspin of emotional and spiritual doubt. Paul talked about this kind of situation in his letter to the Galatians: "Evidently some people are throwing you into confusion and are trying to pervert the gospel of Christ" (1:7).

How do we know which voice speaks the truth? We can know by remembering that God speaks through His Word. Jesus said, "His sheep follow him because they know his voice" (John 10:4).

Ask God to give you more of His voice in your ear. Then listen—with your eyes on the pages of your Bible!

GOD'S LOVE

"By this all men will know that you are my
disciples, if you love one another."
John 13:35

D id you know you're God's special loved one? Do you know why?
When you're saturated in Jesus and God looks at you, He sees His own
precious Son and envelops you in His love for Jesus' sake.

As you and I develop and grow in this love relationship with God,
abiding with Him through meaningful prayer and Bible reading, getting
to know Him on a deeper level as we live out what we say we believe, He
fills us with Himself. We know this because the Bible tells us, "God is love.
Whoever lives in love lives in God, and God in him" (1 John 4:16).

As you and I are filled with God, we will be filled with His love—not
only for Him but for others. The key to loving others is to develop your
relationship with God.

Ask Him to fill your life until you overflow with His love—even for
those you don't like!

LOVE AS JESUS LOVES YOU

Be devoted to one another in brotherly love.
Honor one another above yourselves.
Romans 12:10

When Jesus says we're to "love each other, as I have loved you" (John 15:12), it's a command, not an option!

Jesus' love is totally sacrificial. He defined it in John 15:13: "Greater love has no one than this, that he lay down his life for his friends." He loved us to such an extent that He died for us, irrespective of our condition or response.

Our concept of love seems so much smaller by comparison. We love others who meet our needs, who make us feel good, who do things for us, and who give us things we want. In short, our first concern is having our own needs met.

Jesus outlined a radically different kind of love—a love that puts the needs and well-being of others before our own!

Start putting the needs and well-being of others before your own. Start loving others as Jesus loves you. Why? Because He says so.

No Genie in a Bottle

> At the time of sacrifice, the prophet Elijah stepped forward
> and prayed: "O LORD, God of Abraham, Isaac and Israel, let it
> be known today that you are God in Israel and that I am your
> servant and have done all these things at your command. . . ."
> Then the fire of the LORD fell and burned up the sacrifice.
> *1 Kings 18:36–38*

Prayer may not be easy for you. I struggle with it too. But it's the speaking part of your relationship with God. Think of prayer as conversation. You speak to God in prayer; then you listen attentively as He speaks to you as you read your Bible.

Jesus said, "If you abide in Me, and My words abide in you, you will ask what you desire, and it shall be done for you" (John 15:7 NKJV). Prayer is not like having a genie in a bottle and then rubbing the bottle by faith, hoping the genie will pop out and grant your wish. Prayer is not getting God to do what you want. Prayer is lining up your heart, will, and thoughts with what God wants. Prayer is lining up with God's will.

And how do you know what His will is? By abiding in and trusting and obeying God.

So, no more genie-in-a-bottle prayers! Saturate yourself in God's Word. Then, as you get in step with Him, enjoy talking to God!

THE HOLY SPIRIT'S JOB

Our gospel came to you not simply with words, but also
with power, with the Holy Spirit and with deep conviction.
1 Thessalonians 1:5

Who are you trying to convict of sin? Before my husband moved to Heaven, I can remember that sometimes I would have to bite my tongue to keep from telling him, "You shouldn't do that" or "You shouldn't say that."

My wise mother gave me great advice years ago that I've never forgotten—even if I haven't always taken it! She told me it was my job to make my husband happy, and it was the Holy Spirit's job to make him good. Why is it you and I try so hard to do the Holy Spirit's job for Him? Jesus said, "When [the Holy Spirit] comes, he will convict the world of guilt" (John 16:8).

What a relief! I'm not responsible for making others good. I don't have to judge others as to whether they're good or bad. I'm free to just love and enjoy them.

So let's stop nagging and start praying!

STREAMS IN THE DESERT

Then the angel showed me the river of the water of
life, as clear as crystal, flowing from the throne of
God and of the Lamb.... The Spirit and the bride
say, "Come!" And let him who hears say, "Come!"
Whoever is thirsty, let him come; and whoever wishes,
let him take the free gift of the water of life.

Revelation 22:1, 17

Can you imagine being stranded in the desert with no shade, no water, no nothing? I doubt you'd survive for long. Yet often we live our lives in a *spiritual* desert, separated from God, without the shade of His presence—without the living water of His Word.

Moses challenged God's children to "remember how the LORD your God led you all the way in the desert … to humble you and to test you in order to know what's in your heart" (Deuteronomy 8:2). Are you in a spiritual or emotional desert? A desert of despair? Depression? Doubt? Disillusionment? Could God be testing you … making you thirsty … for Him?

Psalm 107 says He can make streams flow in the desert. So come to Jesus. Drink the living water of His Word.

WHERE'S YOUR SWORD?

Finally, be strong in the LORD and in his mighty
power. . . . Take the helmet of salvation and the
sword of the Spirit, which is the word of God.

Ephesians 6:10, 17

The Bible says the Word of God "is living and active. Sharper than any double-edged sword" (Hebrews 4:12). So where's your sword?

Is it on your mind? In your heart? On your lips? Is it polished from daily reading and study, sharpened and ready to battle our enemy Satan? Have you applied and obeyed its truths in your life? Or is it rusty from lack of use?

If Satan can get us to put down the Word of God—through disregard or disobedience, doubt or denial—he has us right where he wants us, in a very vulnerable position—one in which we will be easily defeated.

Revelation 19:15 says that at the end of human history, Jesus will overcome His enemies once and for all with the sharp sword that comes from His mouth.

Pick up your sword!

Don't Be Intimidated

"Heaven and earth will pass away, but
my words will never pass away."
Matthew 24:35

I'm sure you've heard as often as I have some well-meaning person saying, "It doesn't matter *what* you believe—as long as you're sincere." More often than not, if you don't agree, you're labeled "intolerant," "narrow-minded," or "out of step with reality"!

But the gospel wasn't our idea, was it? Jesus Himself said, "I am the way and the truth and the life. No one comes to the Father except through me" (John 14:6). We come to God through Him—or we don't come at all. The Bible says emphatically that "salvation is found in no one else, for there is no other name under heaven given to men by which we must be saved" (Acts 4:12). That name is *Jesus*!

Share your faith. Present the gospel. And refuse to be intimidated by a world that puts individual perception and opinion over God's Word!

HIS DISPLAY CASE

In this you greatly rejoice, though now for a little while
you may have had to suffer grief in all kinds of trials.
These have come so that your faith—of greater worth
than gold, which perishes even though refined by
fire—may be proved genuine and may result in praise,
glory and honor when Jesus Christ is revealed.

1 Peter 1:6–7

What physical, social, emotional, intellectual, or mental limitation do you have? Instead of blaming it on your doctor or parent or spouse or sibling—or on anyone, for that matter—consider that it might be an opportunity for God to display Himself through your life to others!

The apostle Paul said, "I will boast all the more gladly about my weaknesses, so that Christ's power may rest on me. That is why, for Christ's sake, I delight in weaknesses, in insults, in hardships, in persecutions, and in difficulties. For when I am weak, then I am strong" (2 Corinthians 12:9–10).

God has allowed your weaknesses and limitations as a witness to His power and grace to those who are watching! Hardship is the display case in which God shows off the jewel of your faith. So … let people look and see His glory in you.

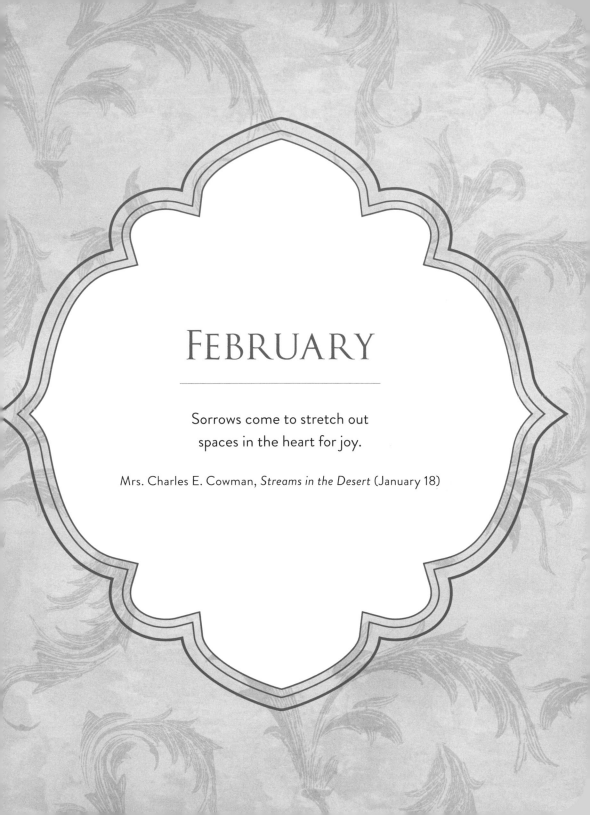

February

Sorrows come to stretch out
spaces in the heart for joy.

Mrs. Charles E. Cowman, *Streams in the Desert* (January 18)

COME TO YOUR FATHER

> One day Jesus was praying in a certain place. When
> he finished, one of his disciples said to him, "Lord,
> teach us to pray, just as John taught his disciples."
> He said to them, "When you pray, say: 'Father.'"
> *Luke 11:1–2*

Here's the good news: Jesus invites you to come. And your entrance into God's presence isn't based on your own worthiness but on the worthiness of Jesus Christ. When you enter God's presence in Jesus' name, you are as accepted by God as Jesus is, because God counts you as His own dear child.

John 1:12 declares, "To all who received him, to those who believed in his name, he gave the right to become children of God." For a child, there's no place quite so safe and secure as within a father's arms. Jesus invites you, in His name, to come into His Father's presence through prayer. Put your head on His shoulder of strength. Feel His loving arms of protection around you. Call Him "Abba"—Daddy.

Don't wait. Come to your Father now.

Talk to Your Brother

If you point these things out to the brothers, you will be a good minister of Christ Jesus, brought up in the truths of the faith and of the good teaching that you have followed.
1 Timothy 4:6

Why is it we're so quick to talk about each other behind our backs? Why do we lack the courage to confront the person we're having a problem with?

Satan must grin wickedly when he sees our gossip disguised as a prayer request or a need to get a third person's opinion. It just adds fuel to Satan's fire as the problem becomes widespread and relationships are damaged.

Jesus commands us, "If your brother sins against you, go and show him his fault, just between the two of you. If he listens to you, you have won your brother over" (Matthew 18:15). Stop talking behind your brother's back and start talking to your brother.

Just Look Up!

Let us fix our eyes on Jesus, the author and
perfecter of our faith, who for the joy set before
him endured the cross, scorning its shame, and sat
down at the right hand of the throne of God.
Hebrews 12:2

My mother told me the story of a former navy officer who kept up his weapons skills to qualify as a deputy sheriff in the county. Each year he was required to renew his permit to keep his status as a deputy. One year, however, he wore new glasses to the target range, and when sweat steamed up his glasses, he totally lost his focus on the target.

When my mother asked, "What in the world did you do?" he quoted the advice of his navy instructor: "When you lose sight of the target, remember your position." He remembered where he'd last seen the target and pulled the trigger. He hit the bull's-eye every time!

Ephesians 1:18 is a prayer that "the eyes of your heart may be enlightened in order that you may know the hope to which he has called you." That hope is Jesus!

Stop looking ahead, looking around, or looking back. Keep your focus on Jesus. Just look up!

GOD'S INITIATIVE

"No one can come to me unless the Father who sent
me draws him, and I will raise him up at the last day."
John 6:44

God always takes the initiative! He took the initiative to create the universe. To create man in His image. To create woman.

God took the initiative to send His own Son to earth to be our Savior. First John 4:19 says, "We love Him because He first loved us" (NKJV).

He took the initiative to draw us to His Son so we could be saved.

He took the initiative when He raised Jesus from the dead and placed the entire universe under His authority.

He took the initiative to send His Holy Spirit to live within us when we receive His Son by faith.

He is taking the initiative now to establish and develop a personal relationship with you, based on His Word. Isn't it time you responded?

CHOICES TO MAKE!

As God's chosen people, holy and dearly loved,
clothe yourselves with compassion, kindness,
humility, gentleness and patience.
Colossians 3:12

How can we possibly put to death our old nature inside us? There are no pills to take, just choices to make. But I can testify from personal experience that you can conquer it one choice at a time, dozens of times a day, every day for the rest of your life.

The choices we make are like a spiritual workout routine. Because I travel so much, I hired a personal trainer to teach me how to use simple elastic bands. Three times a week I try to faithfully exercise certain muscle groups to build up my body strength. The choices we make every day exercise our will like the bands exercise my muscles. They determine whether we will grow spiritually strong or remain spiritually weak. For example, if I choose to lose my temper instead of control it ... if I choose to ignore someone's need instead of meet it ... I've exercised my old nature.

On the other hand, if I control my temper instead of losing it ... if I choose to meet someone's need instead of ignoring it ... I've exercised my new nature.

Start making choices that will develop your spiritual strength. Do it today!

A SPIRITUAL ENGAGEMENT RING

Praise be to the God and Father of our Lord Jesus Christ,
who has blessed us in the heavenly realms with every spiritual
blessing in Christ.... Having believed, you were marked in
him with a seal, the promised Holy Spirit, who is a deposit
guaranteeing our inheritance until the redemption of those
who are God's possession—to the praise of his glory.

Ephesians 1:3, 13–14

When my daughters became engaged, they had beautiful diamond rings. And they thought of a thousand different ways to use their left hands to flash those rings! Before leaving the house, they carefully cleaned their rings. But what really mattered to them was the knowledge that the ring brought with it the pledge of marriage.

The Spirit of God is our spiritual engagement ring. When we receive Christ, He gives us His Spirit as a pledge guaranteeing we'll receive all He has promised, including acceptance by God, forgiveness of sin, and a heavenly home. What a difference it makes when you invite Jesus Christ into your heart—to live within you in the person of His Spirit.

With God's presence in your life, you have the guarantee of all the spiritual blessings in heavenly places. Start naming them, one by one.

OUTPOURING OF BLESSINGS

*Praise be to the God and Father of our Lord
Jesus Christ, who has blessed us in the heavenly
realms with every spiritual blessing in Christ.*
Ephesians 1:3

Regardless of past failures or shortcomings—your relationship with Jesus Christ ensures that what John 1:16 says is true: "From the fullness of his grace we have all received one blessing after another."

When you and I are related to Jesus Christ, our strength and wisdom, peace and joy, and love and hope may run out, but His life rushes in to keep us filled to the brim with one blessing after another. Not because of anything we've done or not done—but just because of Jesus we are showered with blessings.

The Christian life isn't motivated by a list of dos and don'ts but by the gracious outpouring of God's love and blessing. We don't deserve them. Far from it!

We can't earn them.

We can't bargain for them.

And we can't buy them.

They are freely given. Just open up your heart and freely receive them!

A WAKE-UP CALL

In the year that King Uzziah died, I saw the Lord.
Isaiah 6:1

Have you ever slept through your alarm—or found out too late that it didn't go off because you had set it for p.m. instead of a.m.?

When I'm traveling, I have learned that I need actual wake-up calls! And from time to time, I also need spiritual wake-up calls. The daily routine of responsibilities, the never-ending challenge of deadlines, the persistent pressure of problems, and the hectic pace of life tend to preoccupy my thoughts and time with the urgency of the moment. If I'm not careful, I may miss something vitally important that God has for me—something He may want me to see or do—some blessing He wants to give me or wants me to pass along to someone else.

So, He gives me a wake-up call. The call is usually disguised as a crisis or challenge that plunges me to my knees ... where He opens my eyes.

What unexpected, unplanned, unwanted problem or pressure has just invaded your life?

Then this could be your wake-up call. Look up!

THE KEY TO VICTORIOUS LIVING

To be carnally minded is death; but to be
spiritually minded is life and peace.
Romans 8:6 KJV

The Bible is clear that all of us are moral failures. God's Word calls this original, sin-infested nature our "old self" (Ephesians 4:22) or our "sinful nature" (Romans 7:18). This old nature will never please God, and it will never see God. You can learn to manage it, educate it, or drug it, but you can never transform it. Nothing but a brand-new nature will solve the human moral dilemma. Our old natures will never be "cured" of sin, which is why Jesus said, "You must be born again" (John 3:7).

Once you and I are spiritually reborn, we are given a totally new, perfect, sinless nature that is indwelt and empowered by the Holy Spirit.

A supernatural miracle occurs in response to your decision to receive Jesus Christ by faith as your personal Savior and Lord when God places the life of Christ within you. He gives you new emotions to love God and to love people you previously didn't even like, a new will to choose to do what is right and pleasing to Him, and a new intellect to understand the truth and spiritual things.

However, you will always have your old nature to contend with. The key to victory over it is to live intentionally in your *new* nature.

KEEP LOOKING UP

"This is my blood of the covenant, which is poured
out for many for the forgiveness of sins."
Matthew 26:28

God remembers, even when we begin to doubt. God knew that after our salvation experience—while we are trying to live a new life—we would sin again. And because we continue to struggle with sin and failure in our lives, we would be tempted to doubt our salvation.

Hebrews 12:24 tells us that "Jesus [is] the mediator of a new covenant" … a covenant, underwritten by His broken body and poured-out blood. The sign of that covenant is the cross.

When you become so overwhelmed with your own weakness and failure and inability to live a life pleasing to God—look up! Take a good long look at the cross. God loves you with an unconditional love.

Remember that He remembers. You're forgiven!

THE POTTER'S HAND

Yet, O LORD, you are our Father. We are the clay, you
are the potter; we are all the work of your hand.

Isaiah 64:8

God revealed through the prophet, "Like clay in the hand of the potter, so are you in my hand" (Jeremiah 18:6). Under His gentle, loving
touch, your life is molded into a shape that pleases Him. He wants your life
to be useful, and He wants your character to be beautiful. So He places you
in the furnace of affliction until the clay of your life is made strong and all
your colors are revealed—colors that reflect His own character.

Without the loving, skillful touch of the Potter's hand, any usefulness
or beauty the clay might have would be destroyed by the pressure and the
heat. Jesus makes your suffering understandable. His hand is on your life,
developing your faith to display His glory.

He will transform you into a vessel of honor. You can trust your life to
the Potter's hand!

TO BE LIKE JESUS

Those God foreknew he also predestined to be
conformed to the likeness of his Son.
Romans 8:29

I get so tired—*and* frustrated—with my own bad habits. My own sin. I know I've received God's forgiveness for those sins at the cross. *I know that.* But I still sin. I don't want to. I try not to. But I do. The reality of sin is the single most discouraging, defeating fact in my life.

Do you feel defeated by sin too? Second Corinthians 3:18 promises, "We, who with unveiled faces all reflect the Lord's glory, are being transformed into his likeness with ever-increasing glory." That's you and me! We can look forward with hope.

One day, when we get to our Father's house, all our sinful tendencies, sinful thoughts, actions, words, and feelings—all of it—will fall away like a rotten garment that just drops off and is thrown away.

Be encouraged! The character of Christ is being developed in you right now. And one day you'll be like Jesus.

OUR GRACIOUS GOD

The LORD your God is gracious and compassionate. He
will not turn his face from you if you return to him.

2 Chronicles 30:9

Are you disappointed in yourself and shocked by your failure and sin? Are you convinced that while serving God passionately may be a lofty ideal, it's just not attainable? Are you on the verge of going back to your old way of life?

God is gracious to sinners, even those of us who are repeat offenders. There have been times when I knew I deserved God's punishment for my attitude or my actions or my words, but instead, I received His blessing.

Several years ago, I found myself wrestling with a sin that has been a source of struggle and frustration for most of my life. Faced with my repeated failure, I crawled back in humiliation to the foot of the cross, where I expected to hear God tick off, one by one, the dire consequences of my sin or, at the very least, to hear Him sternly rebuke me. Instead, God affirmed His love for me, His promise of blessing, and His call upon my life.

My heart melted! I got up off my knees, and instead of quitting, I passionately recommitted myself to Him. I learned once again, from firsthand experience, that "a bruised reed he will not break, and a smoldering wick he will not snuff out" (Isaiah 42:3).

YOUR FIRST LOVE

"I have loved you with an everlasting love; I
have drawn you with loving-kindness."
Jeremiah 31:3

R egardless of how busy you are "serving" in the church, don't forget
your first love.

Losing it can happen gradually. When you offer yourself for service,
people latch on to your willingness, and, before you know it, busyness over-
takes your worship and love for Jesus. The fire of love for Him you once had
in your heart goes out.

Jesus wrote to the church at Ephesus, warning them, "You have for-
saken your first love. Remember the height from which you have fallen!
Repent and do the things you did at first" (Revelation 2:4–5). The principle
is one we need to remember every moment of every day. Jesus wants our
love for Him before He wants our *work* for Him. Love must come first.

It's love for Jesus that compels you and me to serve from hearts filled
to overflowing. Don't put your work before your worship! Put worship first!

PERSONAL REVIVAL

For this is what the high and lofty One says— he
who lives forever, whose name is holy: "I live in
a high and holy place, but also with him who is
contrite and lowly in spirit, to revive the spirit of the
lowly and to revive the heart of the contrite."
Isaiah 57:15

Considering how strong my love for Jesus is, you would expect my hunger for His presence, my urgent longing to see Him again, to be a constant, motivating force in my life. Yet sometimes in the busyness of my days ... or the duties of my ministry ... or the familiar habits of my worship ... or the everyday routine of my home—the longing becomes complacency, and I sleep through opportunities to be with Him. That's when I most need a wake-up call, a jolt that pushes me to seek out a revival of the passion that began as a blazing, empowering fire but somehow tends to die down to a comfortable but weak, ineffective glow.

The revival I long for is not a tent meeting. It is not a series of church services designed to save the lost. It's a personal revival.

And personal revival is just Jesus ... Jesus in my mind ... Jesus filling my heart ... Jesus overflowing from my life.

So my prayer is, "Just give me Jesus." Please!

SPIRITUAL ENVIRONMENTALISTS

Grace, mercy and peace from God the
Father and from Jesus Christ, the Father's
Son, will be with us in truth and love.
2 John 1:3

Three of the major problems facing us in this millennium are poverty, pollution, and conflict. And the source of these problems is sin in the human heart.

That's why Jesus said, "You must be born again" (John 3:7). We need a new mind to know God and to understand others. We need a new heart to love God and to love others. We need a new spirit of reconciliation with God and forgiveness toward others.

Sin has resulted in wars and conflicts because we don't have peace with God. As a result, we pollute our world with sin, greed, pride, hatred, and prejudice. The solution is God's Son, the only One who can make peace with God and cleanse us of sin.

Be a spiritual environmentalist, someone who helps clean up the pollution of sin. Pray that the world might be reconciled to God; then be reconciled to each other—through faith in Jesus Christ!

TAKING THE FIRST STEP

He took his wife Sarai, his nephew Lot, all the possessions
they had accumulated and the people they had acquired
in Haran, and they set out for the land of Canaan.
Genesis 12:5

Abraham had left Ur not knowing where he was going; yet, when he got to Canaan, he knew he had arrived. He had the deep assurance and conviction that he was exactly where God wanted him to be. He had begun the adventure of stepping out of his comfort zone to truly experience God in a personal, authentic, vibrant relationship.

What a thrilling adventure that is. I recently spoke with a young mother who felt God had called her to accept the incredible challenge to write. As she prayed about it, He confirmed again and again through His Word what she was to do. So, in fear and trembling, she stepped out of all that was familiar and began to put her thoughts on paper.

As she related her experience, she described the thrill of stepping into the flow of God's will and knowing she was exactly where she was supposed to be, doing exactly what she was supposed to do. The intensity of joy in her voice revealed that she had embarked on a magnificent obsession as she experienced God outside of her comfort zone.

How can you arrive in the center of God's will, in the place of the fullness of His blessing, unless you take the first step? Take it. Now!

THE NEXT GENERATION

Even when I am old and gray, do not forsake
me, O God, till I declare your power to the next
generation, your might to all who are to come.
Psalm 71:18

Any relay runner with expertise will tell you that winning the race depends not only on speed but on skillfully passing the baton to the next runner. Are you passing the baton? In the race of life, the baton is the truth that leads to personal faith in God. Each generation receives the baton from the previous generation, and each must pass it on smoothly and securely to the next.

Every day we see advances in longer life spans and expanding knowledge in all kinds of fields. But with all the progress and sophistication, our world is bankrupt of moral and spiritual values. And that moral and spiritual bankruptcy threatens to erode our very existence.

The Bible tells us that God "decreed statutes ... which he commanded our forefathers to teach their children, so the next generation would know them, even the children yet to be born, and they in turn would tell their children" (Psalm 78:5–6).

In the midst of wickedness and waste, pass the baton of truth that leads to personal faith in God to someone in the next generation.

JESUS GIVES MEANING

Though you have not seen him, you love him; and even
though you do not see him now, you believe in him and
are filled with an inexpressible and glorious joy, for you are
receiving the goal of your faith, the salvation of your souls.
1 Peter 1:8–9

Bombarded with bad news everywhere we turn, people are looking for answers. In a world of despair and increasing hopelessness, it's important that you and I not lose our focus. And that focus is *not* on misery, fear, and hate—the problems, crises, or disasters. It's on Jesus. On His forgiveness, freedom, and favor. On the hope that the best is yet to come.

The apostle Peter says that in God's great mercy, "he has given us new birth into a living hope through the resurrection of Jesus Christ from the dead, and into an inheritance that can never perish, spoil or fade—kept in heaven for you" (1 Peter 1:3–4). Jesus gives meaning when life makes no sense. He brings peace in the midst of conflict and gives hope when there is none.

You and I have the Answer: it's Jesus! Now is the time to share the Answer with someone else.

FAITH FOR THE IMPOSSIBLE

"I tell you the truth, if you have faith as small as a mustard
seed, you can say to this mountain, 'Move from here to
there' and it will move. Nothing will be impossible for you."
Matthew 17:20

The couple had longed for a child for decades. *Decades.* Then came the
day when God told Abraham, "As for Sarai your wife, . . . I will bless her
and will surely give you a son by her" (Genesis 17:15–16). Abraham's reac-
tion to the news was so genuinely authentic he was dumbfounded! With
his face pressed against the ground, "he laughed and said to himself, 'Will
a son be born to a man a hundred years old? Will Sarah bear a child at the
age of ninety?'" (Genesis 17:17).

What God had promised was almost beyond belief, and yet as incredu-
lous as Abraham must have felt, he believed. So there was no rebuke from
God for his laughter. Instead, the New Testament says, "By faith Abraham,
even though he was past age—and Sarah herself was barren—was enabled
to become a father because he considered him faithful who had made the
promise" (Hebrews 11:11).

It's encouraging to know that all God required from Abraham was faith
the size of a mustard seed. Abraham's experience teaches you and me that
it's not the amount of our faith that makes the critical difference; it's the
object of our faith. Place the little faith you have in God's Word.

"I FORGIVE YOU"

> Be kind and compassionate to one another, forgiving
> each other, just as in Christ God forgave you.
> *Ephesians 4:32*

Jesus taught His disciples to pray, "Forgive us our debts, as we also have forgiven our debtors" (Matthew 6:12). What a compelling passage of Scripture! God forgives you and me as we forgive others.

If God says, "I forgive you," you must also forgive others, including yourself. His standards are higher than ours. He is more righteous. If God says, "I forgive you," the appropriate response is to say, "God, thank You. I don't deserve it, but I accept it. And to express my gratitude, I forgive that person who has sinned against me, including myself."

We have to forgive because it's what God commands us to do. Our forgiveness becomes an act of worship—one we enter into because of the overwhelming debt of love we owe Him. Choose to forgive yourself and others. Not because they deserve it—but for God's sake.

BRAND-NEW!

> He who was seated on the throne said, "I am making
> everything new!" Then he said, "Write this down,
> for these words are trustworthy and true."
> *Revelation 21:5*

If you live in an old house in need of repair—*brand-new* sounds pretty good. The same is true of an old car that's broken down one time too many. Or a stained carpet. Or cracks in the ceiling.

When we get to our heavenly home, everything's going to be brand-new! Not renovated but created fresh. John emphasized this when he described "a new heaven and a new earth" (Revelation 21:1).

What scars of sin or stains of guilt are you carrying? In your emotions? Your personality? Your relationships? Your memories? Is your life showing the signs of wear and tear?

One day God will wipe away all tears. He'll erase all memories of sin or abuse. Everything—*everything*—will be made new.

FRIENDS WITH GOD

The LORD would speak to Moses face to
face, as a man speaks with his friend.
Exodus 33:11

When I walk with my friend around the lake each morning, we talk about anything and everything: recipes, grandchildren, sales, ball games, politics—whatever happens to be on our minds.

Wouldn't you love to have that kind of free-flowing discussion with the Lord and find out what's on His mind? Is God thinking about stars or planets, black holes or sinkholes, governments or nations, the culture or the church, sin or suffering, demons or angels, hell or heaven, all those big things that He's so good at managing? With so many important things on His mind, it's almost beyond human imagination to even dream that He would have one thought to spare on someone like me. Or you. Yet God reveals what's on His mind to those who make the time to walk with Him as a friend.

Jesus encouraged His disciples to walk with Him when He told them He no longer called them servants, "because a servant does not know his master's business. Instead, I have called you friends, for everything that I learned from my Father I have made known to you" (John 15:15).

Be the friend of God. Listen to His Son.

FORGIVE YOURSELF

If we confess our sins, he is faithful and just and will forgive
us our sins and purify us from all unrighteousness.
1 John 1:9

When I've been tormented by guilt, I've found that I have to talk to God about the reasons for it. I have to get to the bottom of my feelings by confessing my sin specifically by name. I have to confess my failures and mistakes and shortcomings to Him.

Would you do the same? It takes courage not to talk to God in generalities. Be specific. Ask God to forgive you. He promises He will. Then you must—it's not an option, you *must*—forgive yourself.

Think through this with me for a moment: If God says He forgives you, who are you to say, "God, thank You for forgiving me, but I just can't forgive myself"? Are you greater than God? Are you more righteous than He is? Are your standards higher than His?

If He says He forgives us, then you and I have no option but to respond by simply saying, "Thank You. I don't deserve Your forgiveness, but I accept it. I *will* forgive myself . . . for Your sake."

CLEANSED OF SIN

*My dear children, I write this to you so that you will
not sin. But if anybody does sin, we have one who
speaks to the Father in our defense—Jesus Christ.*
1 John 2:1

Isaiah clearly understood that the primary problem in Judah was sin—and
sin is also the primary problem in our world today. Isaiah pleaded with
God's people to repent, quoting God Himself: "'Come now, let us reason
together,' says the LORD. 'Though your sins are like scarlet, they shall be as
white as snow; though they are red as crimson, they shall be like wool'" (Isaiah
1:18). The invitation Isaiah issued was the equivalent of an Old Testament
presentation of the gospel, inviting people to the cross. He knew that God's
people needed to be deeply, thoroughly, completely cleansed of their sin.

Like you and me, Isaiah lived in a world that didn't listen and therefore
just didn't get God's message. Again and again, God warned His people of
impending judgment. Isaiah was committed to preaching God's Word in
an effort to convict God's people of their sin—a conviction that would lead
to repentance, restoration, and a stay of judgment.

While living in a world that is similar to Isaiah's in many respects,
would you commit yourself to Jesus Christ, the living Word of God, and to
the Bible, the unchanging, written Word of God?

BREAK THE CYCLE OF SIN

Therefore, there is now no condemnation for those who are
in Christ Jesus, because through Christ Jesus the law of
the Spirit of life set me free from the law of sin and death.

Romans 8:1–2

It's so hard to acknowledge that, on my own, I have no power to be good in God's sight. But then I'm reminded that all of my righteousness is so permeated with sin that even the best things I could come up with are tainted. The harder I try to be good or to please God, the more I seem to get stuck in my cycle of failure and frustration until I can honestly confess that there is not one good thing in my old nature.

How do we break the cycle of sin and failure?

Victory began for me when I recognized I was in a battle. A battle that would never be won unless I acknowledged my failure to overcome sin. Have you been afraid to confess the strong grip sin has on your life because it makes you feel you're a failure as a Christian? And if you're a failure as a Christian, are you assuming God will not love you or use you?

Don't quit. Return to the cross. Run to Jesus. Confess your sin and failure … again. Ask for cleansing. Ask Him to fill you with His Holy Spirit, the Spirit of life.

THE BRIDE OF CHRIST

"The bride belongs to the bridegroom. The friend
who attends the bridegroom waits and listens for
him, and is full of joy when he hears the bridegroom's
voice. That joy is mine, and it is now complete."

John 3:29

To become Mrs. Danny Lotz, I made my vows of commitment before the eyes of those at our wedding and before God. I vowed to surrender my life and join myself to my late husband, Danny Lotz. He, in turn, vowed to commit himself to me.

My father pronounced us husband and wife. At that point we were married. We signed a certificate that recorded us as officially being married.

When you commit yourself to the Lord Jesus Christ by coming, as it were, to the marriage altar of the cross, you also make vows of commitment to renounce your old life and to love, honor, and obey God as long as you live. Revelation 21:27 says your name is then "written in the Lamb's book of life." It's official!

That registration validates you as an authentic bride of Christ and child of God. Welcome to the family!

Put God's Agenda First

But seek first his kingdom and his righteousness,
and all these things will be given to you as well.
Matthew 6:33

How do you spend your time? Your money? What preoccupies your thoughts?

Jesus said we're to seek first His kingdom and His righteousness. So what's first in your life?

Sometimes when I'm very weary, I give in to the tyranny of the urgent. I allow God to have a secondary place in my life. I sleep through prayer times. I turn down new opportunities for service. I become lethargic about the kingdom of God. When I do, I'm basically in survival mode. And God gets second place.

Is your preoccupation, your weariness, a matter of misplaced priorities? Are you trying to accomplish goals that are not God's? Listen to me! Give careful thought to all your ways. Reorder your life so that God and His agenda are first!

WORTHWHILE CHANGE

The Spirit of the LORD will come upon you in power, and you will
prophesy with them; and you will be changed into a different person.
1 Samuel 10:6

During America's presidential elections, the theme of "change" echoes
in one form or another, from one campaign to another. The idea of
change strikes a chord that resonates with young and old, rich and poor,
men and women, black and white and brown. Thinking of this recurring
need for change, I began to wonder: Is the change that people long for, the
change politicians promise, a change that truly can be delivered? Or are
people who are seeking change confusing the political and the spiritual?
Are they looking for something that only God can give?

The older I get, the more I want things to be familiar. I find myself
choosing the same restaurants to frequent, the same clothing styles to wear,
even the same place to sit in church. Change requires energy that taxes my
strength and mental reserves. So I don't want change just for the sake of
change. I want change that is worthwhile, change I can really believe in.

The good news is that we can believe in the change God brings about
in us through our faith in Jesus Christ. The apostle Paul said, "We live
by faith, not by sight" (2 Corinthians 5:7). Praise God! Change is not only
desirable . . . real change is possible!

MARCH

The "wit's-end" of desperation is the
beginning of God's power.

Mrs. Charles E. Cowman, *Streams in the Desert* (March 25)

I Am Learning

*We have this treasure in jars of clay to show that this
all-surpassing power is from God and not from us.*
2 Corinthians 4:7

I am learning that my faith is more important to God than my feelings are. I am learning that His purpose is to develop my faith for an even greater goal of displaying His glory in and through my life.

I am learning to be at peace, content with whatever transpires, because I know whatever happens is in His hands.

I am learning to die to what *I* want, when *I* want it, and instead choose to trust God to accomplish what *He* wants.

I am learning to stay focused on Him, fulfilling my obligations.

I am learning to love others and care for their needs when my own heart is broken.

I am learning to live with integrity and transparency before others, even when I can't see results.

I am learning to be faithful when my flesh wants to run away.

And as I am learning, I am also praying that God's glory peeps through the cracks in this clay pot.

FOCUS ON JESUS

I know your deeds. See, I have placed before you an open door
that no one can shut. I know that you have little strength, yet
you have kept my word and have not denied my name.
Revelation 3:8

Sometimes we talk about the needs of others or pray about them, even cry over them, but we don't actually do anything to help because we feel so inadequate. When we say, "I can't possibly meet the needs of others; I only have a little time ... a little money," what we're admitting is, "I'm inadequate." We say the same thing when we ask, "What could I possibly do when I have so little ability to make a difference ... a little bit of strength ... a little bit of education?"

If we focus on ourselves, we'll be prevented from serving God, from witnessing, or from living out our lives in risk-taking obedience to Him. When Jesus asked His disciples, "How many loaves do you have?" their answer was a very sheepish, "Seven, ... and a few small fish" (Matthew 15:34). Their focus was on the little bit they had—not on what Jesus could do with it. From that simple offering, Jesus fed five thousand people!

Give Jesus everything you have, even if it's just a little bit. Instead of focusing on how inadequate you feel, concentrate on how big, how capable, how powerful God is.

SATISFACTION AND FULFILLMENT

But we preach Christ crucified; a stumbling
block to Jews and foolishness to Gentiles.
1 Corinthians 1:23

Following his vision of the glory of the Lord, Isaiah humbly made himself available for service. Almost immediately, the assignment was given: "Go and tell this people." His responsibility was to relay the message God gave him to people who would be "ever hearing, but never understanding; be ever seeing, but never perceiving" (Isaiah 6:9).

He was assigned to go to people who would never "get it"! They would be totally unreceptive to the truth. But because he would continue to give them God's Word and they would continue to resist, he would "make the heart of this people calloused; make their ears dull" (Isaiah 6:10). They never would be healed because they never would repent of their sin.

Isaiah was assigned a very tough task!

The success of Isaiah's service would not be determined by the number of people whose lives he changed but by his faithfulness to obey his Lord. In that obedience would come the deep sense of satisfaction, fulfillment, and joy he longed for, rewards he would find as he lived his life to serve and please the One he loved.

God does not command you to be successful. He commands you to be faithful.

NEVER FORSAKEN

"And surely I am with you always, to
the very end of the age."
Matthew 28:20

Jesus is with you—now, and for all eternity—because He lives in you and has promised He'll never leave you or forsake you (see Hebrews 13:5).

When your parents abuse you or leave you through death or abandonment, or your spouse leaves you through divorce, feel the assurance the psalmist knew: "Though my father and mother forsake me, the LORD will receive me" (Psalm 27:10).

When you're facing death, feel comforted by the beloved words of the Twenty-third Psalm: "I will fear no evil, for you are with me" (v. 4).

When circumstances and trials increase in intensity, hear the promises echoed by the prophet Isaiah: "When you pass through the waters, I will be with you" (43:2) and "Neither death nor life, neither angels nor demons, neither the present nor the future, nor any powers, neither height nor depth, nor anything else in all creation, will be able to separate us from the love of God that is in Christ Jesus our Lord" (Romans 8:38–39).

No matter what happens in your life, cling to Jesus. He promises He will be with you forever . . . even to the end of all things.

THE SOLID FOUNDATION OF FAITH

He will be the sure foundation for your times, a
rich store of salvation and wisdom and knowledge;
the fear of the LORD is the key to this treasure.
Isaiah 33:6

Since we live in the midst of a fallen world, we see all around us lives collapsing with broken hearts and shattered emotions, with broken homes and broken hopes.

While we grieve with those who are suffering, we know that the bottom-line problem is that the majority of people in our fallen world are building their lives on a foundation that is cracked and flawed.

The apostle Paul wrote to the Corinthian church, "No one can lay any foundation other than the one already laid, which is Jesus Christ" (1 Corinthians 3:11). There's only one foundation that will last for us, regardless of the pressure or the situation that we might be facing: Jesus! He never changes. And He will never leave you or forsake you.

Do you want to be prepared for the storms of life? Do you want to be able to help others as they are going through these storms? Then first build *your* life on the solid foundation of faith in Jesus Christ—and then share that solid Foundation with others.

STAY CONNECTED

"Remain in me, and I will remain in you. No branch
can bear fruit by itself; it must remain in the vine.
Neither can you bear fruit unless you remain in me."
John 15:4

For your life to bear fruit that pleases God, fruit that has eternal value, you must stay connected to Him. Talk to Him in prayer; listen to Him as you read His Word. Apply to your own life what God says, and then live it out.

If it's a promise, claim it.

If it's a command, obey it.

If it's encouragement, accept it.

If it's a warning, pay heed to it.

If it's an example, learn from it.

Jeremiah 17:7–8 says, "Blessed is the man who trusts in the LORD.... He will be like a tree planted by the water.... Its leaves are always green. It ... never fails to bear fruit." You don't have to try hard to bear fruit any more than an apple tree has to try hard to produce apples. Just stay connected to Jesus.

THE WAY HOME

"I am the way, the truth, and the life. No one
comes to the Father except through Me."
John 14:6 NKJV

Jesus is the truth regardless of culture, age, nationality, generation, heritage, gender, color, or language. We must come to God through Him, or we don't come at all. The Bible says, "God has given no other name under heaven by which we must be saved" (Acts 4:12 NLT).

Think of a wartime paratrooper dropped into the jungle. He thinks he knows the way; but once he lands on the jungle floor, he becomes lost. But then a native guide appears amid the confusing undergrowth, beckons to him, and leads him safely to his base. The guide became the man's way home.

Jesus is God's Guide ready to lead lost sinners safely home. But if you refuse to acknowledge that you are lost and need a guide, you'll never accept God's way. If you resent the fact that there is only one way, you will never follow God's Guide. If you insist on your own way, you will remain lost … forever.

Stop refusing the way, resenting the way, resisting the way … and just follow God's Guide home!

CONNECTED TO THE VINE

"I am the vine; you are the branches. Those who
remain in me, and I in them, will produce much
fruit. For apart from me you can do nothing."
John 15:5 NLT

The branches of a vine live by just remaining connected to the vine. Permanently. Consistently. They simply rest in their position, allowing the sap of the vine to flow freely through them. There's no effort. The fruit is produced by the life-giving sap inside.

When you're completely connected to Christ, His Spirit flows through every part of you—your mind, your will, your emotions, your words, and your deeds. The fruit that you then bear is produced by His Spirit in you. It's not produced by any conscious effort of your own.

If you want to be fruitful, concentrate on your personal relationship with Jesus Christ! "Be filled with the Spirit" (Ephesians 5:18).

TIME FOR GOOD NEWS!

The Spirit of the Sovereign LORD is on me, because the
LORD has anointed me to preach good news to the poor.
Isaiah 61:1

Early in the first century, Judah lived under Roman occupation. The narrow city streets of Jerusalem echoed with the sound of marching Roman soldiers, and the hillsides were dotted with victims hanging on crosses. People were weighed down by bad things. Many people had incurable diseases. The religious system was corrupted by priests appointed by the Roman oppressors. Taxes collected for Rome had reached almost extortion levels. And God seemed silent.

Then one day, in a small synagogue of Nazareth, a young man known as the son of a local carpenter and his wife stood and read from the prophet Isaiah. When He sat down, He announced that Isaiah's words were fulfilled in Him that very day (Luke 4:14–22). He had come to proclaim good news!

In a world of despair and increasing hopelessness, it is important that you and I do not lose our focus. Our focus is not on the despair, misery, and hate. It's not on the problems, crises, or disasters. Our focus is on Jesus and the forgiveness, freedom, and favor that He offers! Saturated in doom and gloom, many people are looking for answers, for something that makes sense of the senseless and gives hope to the hopeless. You and I have the answer—it's Jesus!

MORE OF JESUS

I keep asking that the God of our Lord Jesus Christ,
the glorious Father, may give you the Spirit of wisdom
and revelation, so that you may know him better.

Ephesians 1:17

M y father once asked, "Anne, what do you think revival is?"
Knowing his grasp of church history, I paused to think about my answer.

Daddy added, "Don't you think it may be already happening in your city? Look at what's occurring. Thousands of people are studying the Scriptures for themselves; thousands of people are attending Bible studies and prayer groups. What more could revival be?"

And then I knew the answer. Revival would be *more*.

More people deeply, sincerely repenting of their sin.

More people getting right with God.

More people receiving Jesus.

More people boldly sharing the gospel.

More people serving Jesus.

Revival would just be *more* of Jesus!

If revival is to truly come, it'll be an exclusively God thing. Jesus said to His disciples, "Apart from me you can do nothing" (John 15:5). More blessing and more fruit require more of Jesus.

Revival is just *more* of Jesus!

ASK IN HIS NAME

"In that day you will no longer ask me anything. I tell you the truth, my Father will give you whatever you ask in my name."
John 16:23

My brother Franklin gave the invocation at the inauguration of former president George W. Bush. He led the nation in a prayer for our leaders and their families. He offered his prayer in the name of our Lord Jesus Christ. For days, criticism poured in from the media. They faulted him for praying for the nation yet excluding, they said, those who don't believe in Jesus.

But Franklin wasn't praying to the nation; he was praying to God—on behalf of the nation. And Jesus clearly said, "In that day you will ask in my name.... The Father himself loves you because you have loved me and have believed that I came from God" (John 16:26–27).

Our personal relationship with God's Son, Jesus, is the key that unlocks the door to God's presence ... and to our prayers.

So go ahead. Ask! Pray in Jesus' name. It's your privilege as the Father's child!

JESUS CARES!

The LORD is gracious and righteous;
our God is full of compassion.
Psalm 116:5

Do you think Jesus only cares about things like heaven and hell? About holiness and wickedness? Truth and lies? Jesus does care about those things. But He also cares about your job, whether or not your children do well in school, about your budget, about the roof that leaks and the car that's in need of repair, and the vacation you had to cancel.

The apostle Peter wrote, "Cast all your anxiety on him because he cares for you" (1 Peter 5:7). Jesus cares—even when our problems are of our own making. He cares even if you're having financial struggles because of unwise spending. His caring isn't dependent on what you do.

What are you anxious about? What are your needs today? The needs of your family? The Bible says, "Do not be anxious about anything, but in everything, by prayer and petition, with thanksgiving, present your requests to God" (Philippians 4:6).

Stop worrying and start praying. Jesus cares!

His Name Is Jesus!

And whatever you do, whether in word or deed,
do it all in the name of the Lord Jesus, giving
thanks to God the Father through him.
Colossians 3:17

Elizabeth Carter was a young American woman working in mainland China. One weekend as she hiked up a mountain near her, she saw an old beggar sitting by the path. She passed him by but later regretted it. But as she came down, he was sitting right where he'd been earlier. She went over to him and gently began to tell him that God sent His Son to die on a cross as a sacrifice for the man's sin, and if he placed his faith in God's Son, Jesus, he would receive eternal life. Tears began falling down the old man's face, and he said softly, "I've worshiped Him all my life. I just didn't know His name."

Matthew 1:21 says He was given "the name Jesus, because he will save his people from their sins." Philippians 2:9 says, "God exalted him to the highest place and gave him the name that is above every name."

Don't pass people by. Take a moment to tell them about God's love for them. His name is Jesus!

THE VOICE OF OUR SHEPHERD

> "He calls his own sheep by name and leads them out....
> And his sheep follow him because they know his voice."
> *John 10:3–4*

Sheep today graze in carefully fenced-in pastures and are guarded by specially bred dogs and identified by a number tattooed in their ears. Computers track when they are born and when they are ready for either shearing or slaughter. There is no personal shepherd. Unless the sheep are on a very small farm, even their owner can't tell one sheep from another.

The shepherd of Jesus' day raised his sheep primarily in the Judean uplands. The countryside was rocky, hilly, and filled with deep crevices and ravines. Patches of grass were sparse. So the shepherd had to establish a personal, working relationship with each sheep, developing its love and trust in him to lead it to where the path was the smoothest, the pasture was the greenest, the water was the cleanest, and the nights were the safest. The shepherd always led the sheep. He gave each one a name, and when he called them, they recognized his voice and followed. Their personal relationship with him was based on his voice, which they knew and trusted.

Our relationship with Jesus, the Good Shepherd, is also based on His Voice. He speaks to us through the written words of our Bible. Listen for His Voice as you read His Word. Then follow Him.

WATCH MIRACLES HAPPEN

Our people must learn to devote themselves to doing
what is good, in order that they may provide for
daily necessities and not live unproductive lives.

Titus 3:14

I t's not my problem! How often do you hear that? More important, how
often do you *say* it or *think* it? *Send them away, God. Let the government
take care of them. Let the church do it.*

What are the needs of those around you—in your home, your neighborhood? What would it take to meet those needs? When five thousand people
interrupted Jesus' vacation and stayed all day with Him, they became faint
from hunger. The disciples said, in effect, "Send them away. They're not our
problem."

But Jesus said, "You give them something to eat" (Luke 9:13).

The disciples gave Jesus all they could find—five loaves and two fish. It
wasn't much, but He fed the whole multitude with it.

Don't focus on what you have or don't have. Focus on Jesus. Then give
everything to Him ... and watch miracles happen.

LANDING SQUARELY

I will instruct you and teach you in the way you
should go; I will counsel you and watch over you.
Psalm 32:8

Over the years, I have used four principles I call "runway lights" to help me seek the will of God. Literal runway lights are used to help a pilot guide a plane to a safe landing.

The four "runway lights," or principles, I use to help guide me into the center of God's will when making a decision are (but not necessarily in this order):

- practical circumstances
- the counsel of mature, godly people
- inner conviction
- the confirmation of God's Word

While spiritual "formulas" can sometimes be binding and legalistic, these principles have worked for me so many times, with successful results, that I have used them again and again when seeking God's will.

Since God expects you and me to live in obedience to His will, He will not hide it from us. But He does expect us to prayerfully seek it. Line up the "lights." Then go ahead and land safely.

WALK IN THE LIGHT

When Jesus spoke again to the people, he said, "I am
the light of the world. Whoever follows me will never
walk in darkness, but will have the light of life."
John 8:12

T he best way for you and me to overcome our intimidation and fear of
a hostile culture that surrounds us in our everyday lives is to keep our
focus on the Lord and cultivate an awareness of His presence in our lives.

Not too long ago, I found myself sitting in a select group of people who
were very religious, very self-assured, very articulate—and very unsettling
to me. As we began our discussion, the sun came through the window, and
I could feel it warming my face, almost blinding my eyes. When the conversation began to deteriorate into personal attack, I heard the still, small
voice of God speaking to my heart, *"Anne, 'God is light; in him there is no
darkness at all.... If we walk in the light, as he is in the light, we have fellowship with one another, and the blood of Jesus, his Son, purifies us from all
sin'"* (1 John 1:5, 7). I knew God was affirming that I was in the light ...
literally and figuratively. I was acutely aware that He was with me, and my
fears melted.

So ... step into the Light. And stay there!

YES TO GOD

And we know that in all things God works for
the good of those who love him, who have
been called according to his purpose.
Romans 8:28

To live out God's purpose for your life means there are times when you
have to just say no! Maybe it means saying no to an invitation for dinner in order to keep your commitment at church. No to a lucrative job offer
in order to have more time with your family. No to a long weekend in the
mountains in order to help your neighbor with a challenge he or she is
facing.

It also means there are times to say yes!

Yes to less TV and more study.

Yes to less shopping and more giving.

Yes to less eating and more exercise.

Keep one eye on God's purpose for your life and one eye on your own
purpose for your life. Are they at cross-purposes? Romans 8:28 says we are
called to God's purpose—His will found in His Word.

God isn't something to *add* to your life—He *is* your life! Fully embrace
God's purpose for your life. Don't settle for anything else or anything less.
Say no to self and yes to God.

GOOD OR GREAT?

"Call to me and I will answer you and tell you great
and unsearchable things you do not know."
Jeremiah 33:3

The late Tom Landry was head coach over one of the greatest teams of all time, the Dallas Cowboys. On several occasions, I heard Coach Landry say that during his career he came across many good athletes—but very few great ones. He said the difference between a good athlete and a great one is eighteen inches—the distance from the head to the heart. Good athletes have exceptional ability and a thorough understanding of the game, but great athletes have heart—a passion to play that drives them to selfless sacrifice, brutally long hours of practice, undivided focus, and ultimately, to achieve extraordinary accomplishments.

In over forty years of ministry, I have observed many good Christians—but very few great ones. And the difference is the same eighteen inches—the distance from the head to the heart. While there are many good Christians who have a head knowledge of Scripture and are comfortable with prayer, there are relatively few Christians who are in love with Jesus, who put Him first in their lives when doing so demands that they sacrifice their own time, money, and desires.

How would Coach Landry have described *you*? Are you a good Christian? Or a great one? The choice is yours!

THE REAL THING

To all who received him, to those who believed in his
name, he gave the right to become children of God—
children born not of natural descent, nor of human
decision or a husband's will, but born of God.
John 1:12–13

When you have a smallpox vaccination, the doctor scratches smallpox germs into your skin—just enough for your body to build up immunity against it, just enough of the disease to keep you from catching the real thing.

I know some people who have just enough religion to make them immune to a real relationship with God. They can be the hardest people to reach with the gospel because they are inoculated against it. They've gone to church all their lives and therefore think they are Christians, but they have never truly received Christ.

To have a relationship with God that He accepts, the Bible gives two conditions you and I must meet: we must *receive* Him, and we must *believe* in His *name* (John 1:12). To receive Him means to invite Him to come into your life. To believe in His name means to surrender to Him as Lord, claim Him as Savior, and trust Him as God's Son. Because His name is the Lord Jesus Christ.

Don't settle for religion. Make sure you have the real thing, a personal relationship with God.

CHECK YOUR PILINGS

*No one can lay any foundation other than the
one already laid, which is Jesus Christ.*
1 Corinthians 3:11

Several years ago, my late husband and I asked a contractor to examine the foundation of our house to determine if it was strong enough to withstand new construction. He reported that the pilings had so weakened that anyone who walked across the floor above them risked falling through. Without hesitation, we decided to rebuild the old pilings and thus strengthen the foundation of our home.

The foundation of our society at large, and of our lives in particular, needs to be reexamined too. Is it strong enough for new construction—the advances in science, technology, and medicine that are opening before us in this twenty-first century?

We hear a lot about the "pilings" that we sometimes call "values": family values, ethical values, moral values, medical values, individual values, religious values. But when was the last time you examined them as they undergird the foundation of your own life and family and business? Our culture's generally accepted value seems to be "whatever makes you happy or works for you or feels good," but it makes for a weak foundation.

It's time to check your foundation. Which pilings need to be strengthened, according to God's Word?

KEEP THE FOCUS ON HIM

When my spirit grows faint within me,
it is you who know my way.
Psalm 142:3

Sometimes I publicly share my struggle with a sense of inadequacy so that I might encourage others. But I rarely go into detail, even as a prayer request, because the most well-meaning of my precious friends don't believe me. They argue with me, or they just think I'm being humble. But the feelings of being inadequate can be painful and terrifying, adding enormous stress and pressure to the opportunities for service God has graciously given me.

After more than forty years of serving the Lord outside my home in public ministry, my inadequacy is no longer just a feeling. It's now a fact that I know by experience. I know what I can't do. At the same time, I also know by experience something of what God can do in and through me if I will just make myself available. But for that to happen, I have to get my eyes off of myself and keep my focus riveted on Him.

I have learned that what God calls me to do He also equips me for. He said in Revelation 3:8, "See, I have placed before you an open door that no one can shut." Open doors of opportunity are not options for you or me. He expects us to walk through them, staying focused and dependent on Him.

FAITHFUL

*Let love and faithfulness never leave you; bind them
around your neck, write them on the tablet of your heart.*

Proverbs 3:3

The apostle Philip was put to death for his faith—for sharing the gospel of Jesus Christ. Did he feel it was worth it? There's no record in Scripture that Philip ever doubted what God called him to do. Whether preaching revival in Samaria or leading one Ethiopian eunuch to Jesus, Philip lived his life faithful unto death.

Faithful!

We need to be faithful too.

Faithful to share the hope of the gospel with a co-worker.

Faithful to care for someone in physical need.

Faithful to pray.

Faithful to read God's Word every day.

Faithful to live for Him 24/7 in our own homes, offices, schools, or churches.

It's important that we all be faithful to what God has called us to do.

Why? Because 1 Samuel 26:23 promises, "The LORD rewards every man for his righteousness and faithfulness." Don't miss out on God's reward. Be faithful to Him. Live for Him faithfully ... even unto death!

Don't Forget to RSVP

Believe in the Lord Jesus, and you will be saved—you and your household.

Acts 16:31

If we could work out our own way to heaven, I wonder how many deeds we would have to do to deserve spending eternity there. How perfectly would we have to do those deeds to satisfy a holy God?

Have you been trying to earn heaven? It's impossible! That's why God has given us Jesus. He said, "I am the way and the truth and the life. No one comes to the Father except through me" (John 14:6).

Anyone and everyone is invited to heaven. Anyone and everyone can come. But you must RSVP to His invitation.

Come to Jesus. Put your trust and faith in Him alone.

Not in Jesus plus whatever good deeds you may have done.

Not in Jesus plus your commitment to your church.

Not in Jesus plus all the good things you do.

Jesus alone.

The invitation is clearly issued, once again, at the very end of the Bible: "The Spirit and the bride say, 'Come!' And let him who hears say, 'Come!' Whoever is thirsty, let him come; and whoever wishes, let him take the free gift of the water of life" (Revelation 22:17). It's time to stop trying to impress God. Stop trying to deserve heaven. Just RSVP to His invitation. Now. Tell Him you are coming! Then put your faith in Jesus.

CONFIDENT OBEDIENCE

For you have been my hope, O Sovereign
LORD, my confidence since my youth.
Psalm 71:5

When Abraham and Isaac reached the region of Moriah, "[Abraham] said to his servants, 'Stay here with the donkey while I and the boy go over there. We will worship'" (Genesis 22:5). For three days, as they journeyed, I'm sure Abraham must have thought of nothing other than what God had commanded him to do—sacrifice his only son. He had had time to reflect on all the consequences of what God had said.

If he was going to be bitterly resentful, he had had time for resentment to build in his heart. He could have said, "God, I've been following You for forty years or more, and I can't believe You would 'reward' me like this." Instead, he indicated that giving God his only son was an act of worship.

One of the primary tactics of the enemy is to tempt you and me to doubt God's Word and to doubt God's character. Since the Garden of Eden, Satan has tried to cast God in such a negative light that we lose confidence in who He is and what He has said, and therefore we draw away from Him and disobey Him.

If Abraham was tempted to lose confidence in God, there is no evidence. He just laid his Isaac down—and received heaven's applause!

READY WHEN YOU CALL

Your Father knows what you need before you ask him.
Matthew 6:8

One of the greatest barriers to faith is unwillingness to be made whole—unwillingness to accept responsibility for spiritual immaturity.

Jesus asked the paralyzed man who'd come to the pool of Bethesda to be healed, "Do you want to get well?" The man responded, "Sir, . . . I have no one to help me into the pool.... While I am trying to get in, someone else goes down ahead of me" (John 5:6–7).

The man was focused on what he lacked. He lacked a friend to help him. Lacked the strength to do it on his own. But while he focused on what he didn't have, he overlooked the fact that Jesus was standing right there!

Do you want to get well? What's your excuse for lying down on your responsibilities? For limping in an inconsistent walk? Is it lack of faith? Willpower? Encouragement? If you truly want to be made whole, then look to Jesus. Lean on Jesus. He is right there, ready to help when you call.

SET FREE!

"So if the Son sets you free, you will be free indeed."
John 8:36

Jesus stood before Pilate with blood flowing from His wounds and stream-ing down His face below the thorns in His brow. As part of the Passover celebration, it was Pilate's custom to release any prisoner the crowds chose. The question Pilate asked the crowd changed the course of history: "Which one do you want me to release to you: Barabbas, or Jesus who is called Christ?" (Matthew 27:17). The people shouted, "Give us Barabbas!"

Barabbas? He was a thief and a murderer. To oblige the rioting mob, Pilate set Barabbas free and turned Jesus over to be crucified. As a result, Barabbas became the first person to be set free by the death of Jesus.

But there would be millions of others, including all who believe that Jesus was God's only Son. Including you and me! Hebrews 9:15 says, "He has died as a ransom to set them free from … sins." Free from sin and its penalty. Praise God! Because Jesus died, I've been set free!

ETERNAL LIFE

"For God so loved the world that he gave his
one and only Son, that whoever believes in him
shall not perish but have eternal life."

John 3:16

Are you so overwhelmed with your own weakness, failure, sin, and inability to live a life that's pleasing to God that you've begun to doubt your salvation?

God understands. He knew that after we received Christ, and as we went about living a new life, we would sin again. He knew that, because of the continuing struggle with sin and failure in our lives, we'd be tempted to doubt our salvation.

So God gave us a sign of the new covenant. Jesus confirmed it when He said, "This is my blood of the new covenant, which is poured out for many for the forgiveness of sins" (Matthew 26:28). The sign of the new covenant is the broken body and poured-out blood of Jesus.

It's the sign of the cross.

Take a good, long look at the cross. Remember that God remembers His covenant. Remember He loves you. He's forgiven you. You *are* saved. Forever!

LOVE WITHOUT LIMITS

For I am convinced that neither death nor life, neither
angels nor demons, neither the present nor the future,
nor any powers, neither height nor depth, nor anything
else in all creation, will be able to separate us from
the love of God that is in Christ Jesus our Lord.

Romans 8:38–39

As Jesus came before the crowds just before He went to the cross, Pilate
had Him flogged. History records that flogging victims either went
into unconsciousness from the pain, or they died. The miracle is not that
Jesus survived the beating but that He submitted to it! It would have been
easy for Him to defy those who tormented Him and, in *righteous* judgment,
send them all to hell.

So why would God allow His Son to endure such physical torture? The
answer was given years earlier, when Isaiah solemnly prophesied, "Surely
he took up our infirmities and carried our sorrows…. He was pierced for
our transgressions, he was crushed for our iniquities; the punishment that
brought us peace was upon him, and by his wounds we are healed" (Isaiah
53:4–5).

There are no limits to His love. He shed His blood for you. Look at the
cross and see "I love you" written in red!

OUR DEBT OF LOVE

"Forgive, and you will be forgiven."
Luke 6:37

As Jesus hung on the cross, He cried out, "Father, forgive them, for they do not know what they are doing" (Luke 23:34). Jesus forgave those who nailed Him to the cross.

If Jesus can forgive His executioners, how can you or I withhold our forgiveness from someone else? How can you withhold forgiveness from yourself? If God says, "I forgive you," the only response is to say, "God, thank You! I don't deserve it, but I accept it."

And so, we forgive others, not because they deserve it, but just because He commands it. Colossians 3:13 instructs us to "forgive as the Lord forgave you." Our obedience gives us the opportunity to say to Jesus, "Thank You for forgiving me." Forgive _____ (you fill in the blank) as an act of your worship.

Start paying back the overwhelming debt of love you owe Him! Forgive now.

SOMETHING TO WEAR

Let us rejoice and be glad and give him glory!
For the wedding of the Lamb has come, and
his bride has made herself ready. Fine linen,
bright and clean, was given her to wear.
Revelation 19:7–8

When Jesus finally arrived at the place of execution around nine in the morning, He would have been stripped of all His clothes. Mark 15:24 tells us, "And when they crucified Him, they divided His garments, casting lots for them to determine what every man should take" (NKJV). Yet because Jesus was stripped naked physically, you and I can be clothed spiritually.

The Bible tells us that our righteousness, including the very best things we ever do, is so permeated with sin and selfishness that it is like filthy rags in God's sight (Isaiah 64:6). But at the cross, Jesus gave us His perfect, spotless robe of righteousness, and He took our filthy garments of sin in exchange.

On Judgment Day, you and I will be dressed in His righteousness before God—because Jesus wore the filthy garments of our sin. Praise God! We will be clothed because He was stripped. In heaven, we will have something to wear!

APRIL

In resurrection stillness there is resurrection power.

Mrs. Charles E. Cowman, *Streams in the Desert* (September 3)

TURN TO GOD

I stand in awe of your deeds, O LORD. Renew them
in our day, in our time make them known.
Habakkuk 3:2

When disaster strikes how do we, as God's people, respond?
By weeping?

By giving?

By opening our homes?

By volunteering our time?

As a child of God, there's one thing you can do better than anyone else.
You can *pray.*

The Old Testament prophet Habakkuk set a clear example for you. He
knew the mounting sin in his nation was pushing God beyond the limits of
His patience. God confirmed to Habakkuk that His judgment would fall in
the form of catastrophic disaster. Habakkuk 1:5 says, "Look at the nations
and watch—and be utterly amazed. For I am going to do something in your
days that you would not believe, even if you were told."

Habakkuk turned to God and poured out his heart in prayer.

As you pray, focus on God's availability. On His consistency. On His
glory. On His majesty. On His authority and His sufficiency.

Stay focused on God and pray!

In Jesus' Name

> "Lord, . . . enable your servants to speak your word
> with great boldness. Stretch out your hand to
> heal and perform miraculous signs and wonders
> through the name of your holy servant Jesus."
> *Acts 4:29–30*

We often say we're praying in Jesus' name, but what does that mean? Several years ago I was invited to go to a baseball game by the owner of the club, Jerry Colangelo. When I was halted at the gate by a security guard, I explained I was the guest of Mr. Colangelo, and the gate opened. When I came to the double glass doors, I told the receptionist, "I'm a guest of Mr. Colangelo," and the doors opened. When I went into the stadium itself and said I was a guest of Mr. Colangelo, I was ushered into a private box behind home plate.

I have been to many ball games before and since, but I have never been treated like I was at that one! The difference came because I went in the name of Mr. Colangelo.

Jesus said, "I will do whatever you ask in my name" (John 14:13).

Ask. In Jesus' name.

KEEP IT SIMPLE

The LORD is good, a refuge in times of trouble.
He cares for those who trust in him.
Nahum 1:7

Prayer is so much simpler than we make it! We get bogged down in details. I heard one preacher say, "Don't preach theology to God in your prayers!"

Do we think God doesn't know all the details? All we need to do is tell God our needs, our desires, our feelings, our hopes, and our longings as well as our temptations, our indifference to good, and our taste for evil.

Jesus knew you and I would struggle with prayer. In His parting words to His disciples, Jesus kept it simple. He said, "Ask and you will receive, that your joy may be full" (John 16:24 NKJV).

Tell Him your troubles, your joys, your weaknesses, your needs. Willingly show Him the wounds of your heart.

Ask! Ask Him to help you pray more effectively and with more concentration. Ask Him to help you pray specifically and persistently. Ask, "Lord! Help me to pray!"

ANOTHER KIND OF FREEDOM

Now the Lord is the Spirit, and where the
Spirit of the Lord is, there is freedom.
2 Corinthians 3:17

We're so fortunate to live in a country where freedom is part of our national DNA. Part of our everyday experience. Rarely questioned, and readily enjoyed.

But there's another kind of freedom that isn't bound by national borders or ideology: it's the freedom from sin.

Freedom from spiritual defeat.

Freedom from Satan's traps.

Freedom to reflect Jesus as we're transformed into His likeness.

As you live under the control of the Spirit, the character of Jesus becomes evident to those around you. You reflect what Galatians calls the fruit of the Spirit—love, joy, peace, patience, kindness, goodness, faithfulness, gentleness, and self-control (Galatians 5:22–23).

The Holy Spirit empowers you, not just to *live for* Jesus, but to *be like* Jesus. And therefore to be free at last!

HAPPINESS OR JOY?

We proclaim to you what we have seen and heard, so
that you also may have fellowship with us. And our
fellowship is with the Father and with his Son, Jesus
Christ. We write this to make our joy complete.
1 John 1:3–4

Happiness is often what we *think* we're looking for. But joy is so much better … so much more! Happiness depends more on our circumstances or our things or other people or on our feelings, so we can quickly become unhappy if we lose those things.

But *joy* is rooted in a relationship with God. The Bible says God is the One who will "fill you with all joy and peace as you trust in him, so that you may overflow with hope by the power of the Holy Spirit" (Romans 15:13). And Jesus said to His disciples, "I have told you this so that my joy may be in you and that your joy may be complete" (John 15:11).

Joy that is rooted in Jesus, joy that is rooted in God's Word—why settle for happiness when you can have joy?

ON YOUR KNEES

May my prayer be set before you like incense; may the
lifting up of my hands be like the evening sacrifice.
Psalm 141:2

Are you wearing a mask? Pretending to be more spiritual than you are? When our busy life crowds Jesus out, we cover up. And without even noticing it, we can slip into religious hypocrisy.

Jesus sees right through us. He said to the church at Sardis, "You have a reputation of being alive, but you are dead" (Revelation 3:1). There was a time in my life when Jesus rebuked me through the words of this letter to the church at Sardis. I had a reputation for being alive. I could lead people to faith in Jesus. Yet He said, "Anne, on the inside I see you're dying." The reason? Prayerlessness. He told me what He told Sardis: "Wake up! Stop neglecting prayer."

Do you need blanket victory—victory over those blankets in the morning? Wake up! And get down on your knees.

A WORLD OF PRIVILEGE

"You may ask me for anything in my name, and I will do it."
John 14:14

When you come to God through prayer, believing in Jesus' name, you enter a world of privilege! Doors open, mountains move, doubts disappear, and fears fade.

Jesus says in John 15:16, "The Father will give you whatever you ask in my name." The God of the universe bends down to hear what you have to say. And He answers.

You don't have to go through a religious leader. You don't have to check with a secretary. You don't have to be in church. You don't have to make a donation. And God isn't concerned with where you live or how much money you make or how brilliant or eloquent you are.

Prayer is as simple as talking to God—in Jesus' name!

STRUGGLING WITH PRAYER?

After Jesus said this, he looked toward heaven
and prayed: "Father, the time has come. Glorify
your Son, that your Son may glorify you."
John 17:1

One of the greatest privileges we have in Jesus Christ is the privilege of actively communicating with the God of heaven. Yet often I struggle in prayer. I struggle with the content, with consistency, and with keeping my concentration focused.

Are you struggling in your prayer life also? In making time for prayer? In knowing how to pray? Or in getting answers to prayer?

Prayer is the single greatest struggle of my Christian life. I don't wrestle *in* prayer as much as I wrestle *with* prayer. Attitude has everything to do with prayer. My attitude needs to be that I want what God wants more than what I want.

The entire bottom-line reason for prayer is that God be glorified, that God be revealed in and through us and in that for which we pray.

Won't you join me in prayer?

Pray when you feel like it. Pray when you don't feel like it. Pray until you do feel like it!

DO WHAT HE SAYS

> His mother said to the servants, "Do whatever he tells you."
> *John 2:5*

When you pray for your marriage, or for any difficulty you're having, *how* do you pray? Do you tell God how to fix what's wrong?

In John 2:3, Mary was attending a wedding with Jesus and others, and she said to Him, "They have no more wine." Just a simple acknowledgment of the problem. Could you do what Mary did?

Jesus' answer to Mary might seem strange to you. He said, "Why do you involve me?" (v. 4). I believe it's Jesus' challenge to us to search our hearts for hidden motives as we pray for help.

Are we asking because we're tired of feeling bad? Are we asking for a better job because we want more prestige?

Jesus knows your struggles. He knows how difficult it is not to feel loved, the frustration of making ends meet. The bottom line—in whatever you do—is to glorify God! First, last, and always!

HE CARES FOR HIS SHEEP

Know that the LORD is God. It is he who made us, and
we are his; we are his people, the sheep of his pasture.
Psalm 100:3

People were never an interruption to Jesus! They were an opportunity to show His loving care and His Father's compassionate power to meet their deepest needs. Why? Because He made us, and we are the sheep of His pasture.

Jesus cares about you, about your job, about your children, about college tuition, about the car that's broken down, the roof that leaks, and all the physical problems and needs you're facing. It's the very nature of a shepherd to care for His sheep.

Jesus said, "I am the good shepherd" (John 10:11). When He saw a large crowd, He saw that they were like sheep without a Shepherd, and He had compassion on them. There's nothing in your life—past, present, or future—that Jesus is not concerned with. He cares!

NEVER DOUBT GOD'S LOVE

God demonstrates his own love for us in this:
While we were still sinners, Christ died for us.

Romans 5:8

Do you doubt the love of God? Why? Because of the bad things He allows to happen? Because of the unfairness and injustice you see around you? The misery and suffering and pain and cruelty of life?

Some questions won't be answered until you get to heaven. But one thing you can know for sure is that God loves you! How do you know it's true? John 3:16 says it in a nutshell: "God so loved the world that he gave his one and only Son."

We know it's true by just looking at the cross where Jesus proved His love for the world that mocks Him, and ignores Him, and despises Him, scorns Him and rejects Him.

Look at the cross and see "I love you" written in Christ's blood. Jesus has come to meet your every need!

SUNDAY IS COMING!

In a loud voice they sang: "Worthy is the Lamb, who
was slain, to receive power and wealth and wisdom
and strength and honor and glory and praise!"
Revelation 5:12

I n my own life I have a promise from God's Word that I've continually claimed in prayer. There's absolutely nothing I can do to hasten or help God fulfill His promise and answer my prayer. My dependence is on God, and God alone.

It's why the angel's pronouncement at Christ's resurrection is so thrilling: "He is not here; he has risen, just as he said. Come and see the place where he lay" (Matthew 28:6). The resurrection on that first Easter Sunday had been preceded by the cross on Friday and the tomb on Saturday. In other words, God's most powerful work is often preceded by our utter hopelessness and helplessness.

Which day of the week is it in your life? Is it Friday and you're experiencing the death of a promise? Is it Saturday and you're filled with a numb hopeless, helpless despair? Listen to me. Place all your faith in God alone—Sunday is coming!

HE'S ANGRY TOO!

Why are you downcast, O my soul? Why so
disturbed within me? Put your hope in God, for I
will yet praise him, my Savior and my God.
Psalm 43:5

When tragedy strikes, so often we lash out in anger toward God. But you know, He's angry too.

Instead of being angry at God, direct your anger toward sin and its devastating consequences of suffering and death. Our hope is in knowing there's genuine, triumphant, permanent victory over it! It's available through Jesus Christ. Let that be your witness, your testimony of God's grace.

When Jesus came to the tomb of His friend Lazarus, He "was deeply moved in spirit and troubled" (John 11:33). He was angry—angry at the temporary victory death had over life. But He knew, better than anyone, that death's victory was short-lived because resurrection was coming.

Don't focus on the tragedy and death. Focus on the empty tomb. Put your hope in the One who is the Resurrection and the Life.

THE ULTIMATE BLESSING

Be exalted, O LORD, in your strength; we
will sing and praise your might.
Psalm 21:13

Jesus is your risen Lord and reigning King. The Bible says you're not your own. You belong to Him, and He wants to share His glory with you!

I can't think of anything more thrilling. It means you no longer live by what you *want* but by what He *says*. Psalm 21:5–6 says, "You have bestowed on him splendor and majesty. Surely you have granted him eternal blessings and made him glad with the joy of your presence."

The blessing He'll give you isn't necessarily more wealth. Or even good health or any kind of material prosperity. It's not like rubbing a genie's lamp and waiting for your requests to be granted.

The ultimate blessing God wants to give you is summed up in one word: *Jesus!* If you want more blessing, you're asking for more of Jesus!

PRECIOUS IN HIS SIGHT

But if anyone obeys his word, God's love is truly made
complete in him. This is how we know we are in him.

1 John 2:5

The prayer in Psalm 139:1–2 says, "O Lord, you have searched me and
you know me. You know when I sit and when I rise; you perceive my
thoughts from afar." What a relief that Jesus knows who we are. In fact, He
knows us so well He understands that apart from Him, we can do nothing.

You don't have to prove yourself to Him. You don't have to worry about
disappointing Him. You don't have to earn His respect. You don't have to
work hard to be accepted. You don't have to produce a quota. You don't
even have to be successful. God says, "You are precious and honored in my
sight, and ... I love you" (Isaiah 43:4).

God loves you! *God loves you!* You are precious to Him. And nothing
can ever separate you from His love. Nothing—not even yourself!

YOU ARE IMPORTANT

> "I am the good shepherd; I know my sheep and my
> sheep know me—just as the Father knows me and I know
> the Father—and I lay down my life for the sheep."
> *John 10:14–15*

The most important Man in the universe thinks you're so important that He gave His own life for you. Jesus said, "I have come that they may have life, and have it to the full" (John 10:10).

It's difficult to be depressed over the smallness of life when you realize that Jesus died for you, has given you everlasting life, and will one day return for you. Your life has value. You are His treasure! You can find encouragement and hope and purpose to live through Jesus Christ.

Jesus is your provider. Your strength. Your help. When you struggle with sin, when you're inconsistent, or stumble, or fail . . .

He is the Savior who has redeemed you.

The Lord who rules your life.

The King who will return for you.

Thank Him for who He is and for what He has done because He loves you.

HAVE YOU FORGOTTEN?

*He was despised and rejected by men, a man of sorrows,
and familiar with suffering. Like one from whom men hide
their faces he was despised, and we esteemed him not.*
Isaiah 53:3

Imagine what it would be like to be on trial for something you didn't do, and not one person stands up in your defense.

One of the most tragic scenes to me in all of Scripture is when Jesus was arrested in the Garden and placed on trial. Many accusers blamed Him for treason—but where was the blind man He'd given sight? Where was the leper He had cleansed? The adulterous woman He had forgiven? Where were they? John 12:19 says, "Look how the whole world has gone after him!" Yet not one stood with Him at the end. Did they forget?

Have *you* forgotten what Jesus has done for you too?

Take a moment today. Make a list of what Jesus has done for you. Add to it every night before you go to bed. Then thank Him for what He has done by living your life identified with Him.

JUST TO LOVE HIM

God is love. Whoever lives in love lives
in God, and God in him.
1 John 4:16

In India, Amy Carmichael founded a home for young girls who had been sold as prostitutes. Their life expectancy was no more than twelve years. She rescued as many as she could, raising them in a Christian home. It must have seemed like the Garden of Eden to those young girls.

One day a little girl stood shyly at Miss Carmichael's desk and said quietly, "I have come."

Miss Carmichael stretched out her arms to welcome her and gently asked, "Why have you come?"

She said softly, "Just to love you."

Jesus said to His disciples, "The Father himself loves you" (John 16:27). Like the little Indian girl, God has drawn near to us in the person of His Son, Jesus, to simply say, "I love you."

The Way Up Is Down

"If anyone would come after me, he must deny
himself and take up his cross and follow me."
Matthew 16:24

Success. Position. Power. They're part of the edict of the culture we live in. And yet God's blessing in your life and mine comes in direct proportion to the extent you and I are willing to give up our will, our goals, our dreams to His will. Nothing is more countercultural than that!

It's what Jesus meant when He challenged His disciples to take up their crosses and follow Him. The Bible says Jesus endured the cross, scorning its shame, and sat down at the right hand of the throne of God—blessed by God with a position of power and authority.

Follow Jesus. He will lead you to a cross. But remember that after the cross come the resurrection and the power and the glory and the crown! That's why the way up ... is down.

TAKE HIS HAND

In love he predestined us to be adopted as his sons
through Jesus Christ, in accordance with his pleasure
and will—to the praise of his glorious grace, which
he has freely given us in the One he loves.
Ephesians 1:4–6

A boy named Geoffrey heard that evangelist D. L. Moody was to preach. He walked all day to get to the church where the great man was to speak. But when he was about to enter, a doorman noted Geoffrey's unwashed face and shabby clothes and said, "You're too dirty to go inside!"

Just then a distinguished-looking man arrived. Seeing tears on the boy's face, he asked, "What's wrong?"

Geoffrey blurted out, "I came to hear Dr. Moody, but they said I'm too dirty to go inside."

"Here, take my hand. Come with me," the man told him.

Geoffrey took the man's hand and was led inside—where he was seated in the front row! The man then walked to the pulpit and began to preach! Geoffrey had held the hand of D. L. Moody—the only reason he had been accepted inside the church.

Jesus offers His hand at the cross. Take it. You will be welcomed and accepted in His heavenly home.

God Loves You!

I trust in God's unfailing love for ever and ever.
Psalm 52:8

When our loving God looked down and saw our helplessness, our hopelessness, He did something about it. He came down from heaven in the person of Jesus Christ. He got involved in the lives of those flooded with sin and its consequences.

He gave us Living Water to satisfy our thirst for fulfillment and meaning and happiness.

He gave us the Bread of Life to strengthen and sustain us on our life's journey. He shed His own blood to wash away the filth of our sin. He rose from the dead to give us brand-new life.

Listen to me: God loves you! Stop doubting His love and simply receive it. Then say thank You, and love Him in return.

The Risk of Faith

> "Come," [Jesus] said. Then Peter got down out of the
> boat, walked on the water and came toward Jesus.
> *Matthew 14:29*

The older I get, the less I want to take risks. How about you? In today's financial world, that's probably a wise thing. But a cautious attitude in your spiritual life can cause you to procrastinate to the point you become disobedient.

God has not given us a "spirit of timidity, but a spirit of power" (2 Timothy 1:7). Living a life of faith requires taking risks, from our perspective, because we can't physically see what lies ahead, hear audibly what God's saying, or know what He's thinking. We have to trust Him as we choose to give Him our children, our jobs, our homes. Even our comfort.

Learn from Peter. He never would have known he could walk on water if he hadn't stepped out of the boat.

Discover the power of God. Step out of your comfort zone. Take the risk of faith.

PUNISHMENT FOR SIN

The son will not share the guilt of the father, nor will
the father share the guilt of the son. The righteousness
of the righteous man will be credited to him, and the
wickedness of the wicked will be charged against him.
Ezekiel 18:20

At the end of a class, a young woman, obviously distraught, approached me. She was convinced she'd had a miscarriage because God was punishing her for some sin she'd committed.

I shared with her the words above from the prophet Ezekiel. That distraught mother smiled through her tears, as she was reassured that God had not taken the life of her baby as judgment for her sin.

Our children may suffer the consequences of our sins, but God will never punish them for anything we might have done. God has already punished His own Son for your sins and mine!

STAY ALERT!

Stand firm then, with the belt of truth buckled around
your waist, with the breastplate of righteousness in
place, and with your feet fitted with the readiness
that comes from the gospel of peace.
Ephesians 6:14–15

In recent years our eyes have been opened to a hate-filled enemy who uses terrorism to achieve the goal of destroying us. We're often put on alert with warnings of danger, and our military and intelligence agencies operate on full alert twenty-four hours a day around the world. Similarly, as a Christian, you have a deadly enemy, the devil, who has even deadlier intentions. He's dedicated to your utter destruction.

Ephesians 6:11 warns, "Put on the full armor of God so that you can take your stand against the devil's schemes." God's Spirit puts us on alert, warning us of the danger we face. Are you experiencing difficulty in your health? Your relationships? Your job? Your finances? Could the difficulty be the enemy's attack?

Stay alert! And be assured: the Bible says the One in you—Jesus—is greater than the one who is in the world. Victory is yours!

PERMANENTLY DELETED

As far as the east is from the west, so far has
he removed our transgressions from us.
Psalm 103:12

Sometimes, as I work on my computer, the promise of Psalm 103:12 comes to mind when there are files or folders I want to throw away. In order to discard them, I have to drag them to the trash can on my screen. Then I hit the delete button. A little window pops up and asks if I'm sure I want to delete the trash, and when I affirm that I do by hitting the button a second time, the trash disappears. Totally. Permanently. I can't retrieve it, even if I try.

When you and I confess our sin and come to the cross, we are cleansed with the blood of Jesus. It's as though God drags our sin to the heavenly trash can, hits the delete button, and it's gone! As far as the east is from the west, it's been removed. And if you think about it, the east is as far removed from the west as it's possible to be, since the two will never meet!

When I come to God humbly, through faith in Jesus, He erases my sin from His memory much more effectively than I erase things from my computer. My sin is permanently deleted.

COMING GLORY

I consider that our present sufferings are not worth
comparing with the glory that will be revealed in us.
Romans 8:18

The truth is—bad things happen to those Jesus loves. Audrey Wetherell Johnson was born in England and educated in Europe. She was an agnostic but was transformed by God's grace into a gifted Bible teacher. In the 1930s, she felt God calling her to be a missionary.

After years of teaching in a seminary in a foreign country, Miss Johnson was captured with other missionaries and placed in a concentration camp for three years of unimaginable suffering. When Miss Johnson was finally released, she came to America and began Bible Study Fellowship—an international ministry impacting millions of people to study God's Word each week.

When something bad happens to you—look forward to the glory that is coming!

THE TRICYCLE APPROACH TO LIFE

"I am the LORD your God, who teaches you what is best
for you, who directs you in the way you should go."
Isaiah 48:17

A lot of us have what I call "a little red tricycle" approach to life!
One year we bought a red tricycle for our daughter. My husband pulled
the pieces out of the box and said, without reading the directions, "Anybody
can put wheels on." But, when he finished, every wheel was angled in a different direction!

Some of us treat life as though it's so simple we don't need directions.
Until life doesn't work—and then we wonder what's gone wrong.

Your life *did* come with directions. Don't ignore them!

Broken lives, broken dreams, broken families, broken hopes? God never
intended you to be broken! Follow His directions. You'll find them in the
Bible.

SOMEONE TO CARE FOR

The God of all grace, who called you to his eternal glory in
Christ, after you have suffered a little while, will himself
restore you and make you strong, firm and steadfast.
1 Peter 5:10

D o you ever think, *Poor me! No one has it as bad as I do! No one has my schedule, my pressures, my difficulties. No one cares about me. And right about now, I wouldn't blame them if they didn't care?*

The truth is, you and I accentuate our pain when we dwell on it all the time. We become self-centered. But there's a way to overcome the pain, the depression—and that's to focus on the needs of others.

First John 4:7 says, "Let us love one another, for love comes from God. Everyone who loves has been born of God and knows God." Who do you know who's suffering and could use your encouragement? What can you do to ease that person's load?

Ask God to bring to your attention today someone to care for. Find the joy in easing his or her burden, and in the process, you'll ease your own.

DIRT ON OUR HANDS

He poured water into a basin and began to
wash his disciples' feet, drying them with the
towel that was wrapped around him.
John 13:5

In the midst of the suffocating nightmare of losing a child, a friend of mine desired that God would be glorified. She asked me to pray for her loving patience and thoughtful sensitivity. She was asking me to pray for more of Jesus' dirt on her hands!

Just what is His dirt on our hands? It's serving others when *you* need to be served. Praying for others when you need to be prayed for.

Getting our hands "dirty" with more of Jesus in your life is illustrated wonderfully by Jesus' example on the night He was betrayed, just before His crucifixion. Jesus took His disciples to an upstairs room, where the Bible says He served them! Their "dirt" was on His hands.

When you're overwhelmed with problems and pain, get involved in the needs of others. Drop to your knees and cry out to God, "Give me *more* of Your dirt on my hands!"

WHEN THE HEAT IS TURNED UP

In this you greatly rejoice, though now for a little while
you may have had to suffer grief in all kinds of trials.
1 Peter 1:6

Sometimes God turns up the heat!

A friend told me about a gift he received. It was a box with lots of little compartments for different flavored teas. The compartments were labeled; the tea was not. One morning, groggy with sleep, he reached for the tea box. It fell, scattering tea bags all over the floor. He had no idea which was Earl Grey and which was lemon mint. So, each morning after that incident became a "surprise tea" adventure. He never knew which flavor he'd enjoy until the heat of the water drew it out.

Are you feeling the heat of pressure, problems, and stress right now? God may use heat to draw out the "flavor" of your character. Listen to me: 1 Peter 1:7 says that "these have come so that your faith ... may be proved genuine ... when Jesus Christ is revealed."

So ... when the heat is turned up, make sure the flavor that comes out is *Jesus*.

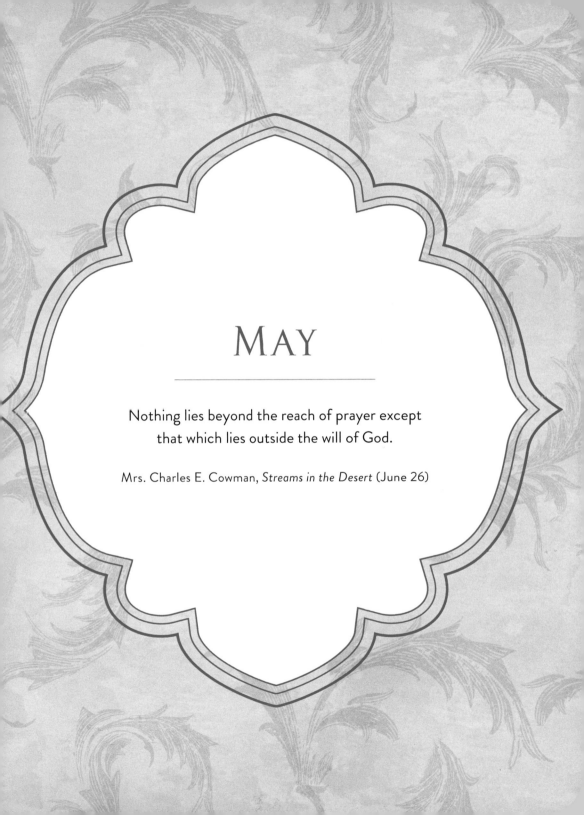

MAY

Nothing lies beyond the reach of prayer except
that which lies outside the will of God.

Mrs. Charles E. Cowman, *Streams in the Desert* (June 26)

HOPE FOR THE FUTURE

He mounted the cherubim and flew; he
soared on the wings of the wind.
Psalm 18:10

In the whirlwind of life, I'm sometimes an emotional turkey. They say in a storm a turkey reacts by running under the barn, wings over its head. In contrast, an eagle, when it senses a storm coming, spreads its wings and allows the wind to carry it higher. Well, I'm one who wants to be an eagle but sometimes feels like a turkey!

What storm has swept into your life? Death? Divorce? Disease? A betrayal? I'm convinced God allows storms to increase and intensify in our lives because He wants us to soar higher in our relationship with Him—to grow stronger in our faith, to bear more fruit in our service to Him. In Matthew 8, a furious storm arose when Jesus and His disciples were in a boat on the lake. In a panic, the disciples went to Jesus and said, "Lord, save us! We're going to drown!"

He replied, "You of little faith" (vv. 25–26).

Then He spoke to the storm and brought peace.

I'm convinced that storms are coming. What are you doing to prepare?

I encourage you to spread your wings of faith through daily Bible study, disciplined prayer, and obedience to God. Keep your focus on Jesus as you ask Him to enable you to soar higher.

OUR OWN WORST ENEMY

He has not despised or disdained the suffering
of the afflicted one; he has not hidden his face
from him but has listened to his cry for help.
Psalm 22:24

We're often our own worst enemy when it comes to suffering. Headaches and stress can be made worse by bitterness or anger. We can be injured in a car accident by choosing to disobey a signal or a law of the road. So it's a legitimate response to examine ourselves before God to determine if we're suffering because of personal sin or because of someone else's sin.

Yet your suffering may be no one's fault.

John 9:1–3 describes a situation when Jesus' disciples were sure the man's handicap was someone's fault. Jesus said, "Neither this man nor his parents sinned,... but this happened so that the work of God might be displayed in his life" (v. 3).

God's grace and power seem to reach their peak when we're at our weakest. You can glory in your weakness and rejoice in your suffering because it gives God an opportunity to display His work in your life.

GRACE AMID GRIEF

I delight greatly in the LORD; my soul rejoices in
my God. For he has clothed me with garments of
salvation and arrayed me in a robe of righteousness.

Isaiah 61:10

Several years ago, a fighter jet crashed into a neighborhood yard, killing a wife and mother who lived there. It was a tragedy beyond imagination. And yet the woman's husband expressed to news media how concerned he was for the safety of the pilot, who, by the way, survived the crash. He said, "It wasn't his fault. This young man is defending our country. We need to support him all we can." This anonymous man was quiet-spoken, but his amazing response spoke loudly of compassion and grace amid grief.

Keep his response in mind when you consider who is praising Jesus right now because you are.

The light we are in this world will grow dim if it's interrupted by our criticism and complaints, our selfishness or indifference, our insistence on our own interests.

When we praise God in the most difficult circumstances, it causes others to do the same. Praise Him. And keep on praising Him!

A Pleasing Aroma

For we are to God the aroma of Christ among those
who are being saved and those who are perishing.
2 Corinthians 2:15

I hadn't seen Brad for a year. He'd been battling cancer, so when he arrived at our home, I was very happy to see him. The dark circles under his eyes were evidence of his recent radiation and chemo treatments. But he gave me a wide grin when I asked how he was doing.

He said, "Mrs. Lotz, God has been so faithful to me. He's brought me to the point where I can work again. He's put my cancer in remission. He's even giving me my next breath!"

When Brad left that day, the fragrance of his life filled my house. The experience reminded me of Exodus 29:18, which says the priests consecrated their sacrifice as an "offering to the LORD, a pleasing aroma, an offering made to the LORD by fire."

Has God placed you in the fire? Then live your life as an offering, a pleasing aroma to God.

GOD'S PRECIOUS GEMS

These have come so that your faith—of greater worth
than gold, which perishes even though refined by
fire—may be proved genuine and may result in praise,
glory and honor when Jesus Christ is revealed.

1 Peter 1:7

Could it be God has given you a platform of suffering so you can be a witness of His power and grace to those who are watching?

If we feel good and look good, if our home is always orderly, our boss is always pleased, our bank account is always sufficient, and we're always patient and kind—well—that's not so inspiring, is it? But if you have a splitting headache, the kids are screaming, and your cell phone's ringing—and you're patient, kind, thoughtful, loving in the midst of those challenges—then the world sits up and takes notice. It's just not natural. It's supernatural.

Suffering gives God opportunities to work for His glory. The Bible says these situations come so your faith can be demonstrated as genuine and Jesus' presence in your life can be revealed. Your suffering can be a gleaming showcase for displaying the precious gems of God's character reflected in you.

SERVING SELF OR OTHERS?

Having loved his own who were in the world, he
now showed them the full extent of his love.

John 13:1

What enormous needs do you have? What crisis are you facing? As a result of the difficulties in your own life, have you backed off from serving others? Maybe you've lost touch to the extent you don't even know the needs of those around you, perhaps including those in your own home.

Isn't it amazing how pain and pressure can so totally preoccupy our attention they make us completely self-centered? Jesus, on the night He was betrayed, when He knew His time had come to go to the Father, sat with His disciples and showed them His love. Then He washed their feet.

There couldn't have been a more inconvenient time for Jesus to serve others—but He did!

Serve others even when it isn't convenient. It's one secret to overcoming the problems in your own life.

NOT MY WILL

> "Father, if you are willing, take this cup from
> me; yet not my will, but yours be done."
> *Luke 22:42*

What is the hidden agenda in your prayers? Are you praying for God to save your marriage to avoid humiliation? Are you asking for physical healing because you're tired of feeling bad? Are you asking for a better job because you want more prestige?

James 4:3 says, "When you ask, you do not receive, because you ask with wrong motives." When we pray, He wants us to search our hearts for hidden motives—not just in praying for ourselves, but in praying for others. Why are we *really* asking for help? If your marriage is broken, if your finances are depleted, if your children are turning their backs on you and God—what is it that you truly want from God? Tell Him what you want. Then qualify your prayer, as Jesus did, with, "Thy will be done" (Matthew 6:10 KJV).

ON THE WINGS OF A STORM

The LORD looks down from heaven on the sons of men to
see if there are any who understand, any who seek God.
Psalm 14:2

A dear friend described some pretty significant testing. She said in less than twelve months, she'd seen her health fail, her property damaged, a close friendship threatened—all while her workload at the office escalated. Her story illustrates how life-shaking experiences can prepare us for a fresh encounter with God. For my friend, it was a year that triggered a personal revival.

Sometimes only adversity can accomplish that kind of revival.

The Old Testament prophet Ezekiel related that as a captive to King Nebuchadnezzar, "I looked, and I saw a windstorm ... an immense cloud with flashing lightning and surrounded by brilliant light" (Ezekiel 1:4). But on the wings of that storm, God brought Ezekiel an important message, a wake-up call to a fresh vision of Jesus.

When the storm comes, look up for personal revival!

BIGGER THAN YOUR FEARS

A righteous man will be remembered forever. He will
have no fear of bad news; his heart is steadfast, trusting
in the LORD. His heart is secure, he will have no fear.

Psalm 112:6–8

Who of us hasn't spent nights tossing and turning? Nights when we look at the clock, and it barely moves? We lie there mulling over situations and issues, most of which we can do nothing about—but fearful of the outcome.

In John 14:1, Jesus says, "Trust in God; trust also in me." The answer to fear . . . is faith. When I'm fearful for a loved one or for something that's coming up in my life, I'm comforted and calmed as I meditate on who God is. It helps me plant my faith in someone bigger than my fears.

The next time fear overwhelms you, think about who God is. Look for a Scripture verse that underscores God's characteristics. Then consider your situation in light of who He is.

Trust in God. He will never fail you, leave you, or forsake you. You can count on Him!

IS GOD LOOKING FOR YOU?

> "Again, the kingdom of heaven is like a
> merchant looking for fine pearls."
> *Matthew 13:45*

God is looking for a few good men and women. Men and women who are willing to go against the current of popular opinion, to hold firm convictions in a world where "anything goes," to speak the truth when it's not politically correct, and to walk with God when everyone else is running away from Him.

God is looking for those who believe that what He says is more important than what anyone else says. He's looking for people who know that what He thinks is more important than what anyone else thinks, and that what He wants is more important than what anyone else wants. God is looking for those who believe His will is more important than their own.

Second Chronicles 16:9 says, "The eyes of the LORD range throughout the earth to strengthen those whose hearts are fully committed to him." God is looking for another Noah. Another Abraham. Another David. Another Daniel. Another Peter or another Paul.

Are *you* one God is looking for?

PEACE IN THE WORLD

He will be called Wonderful Counselor, Mighty God,
Everlasting Father, Prince of Peace. Of the increase
of his government and peace there will be no end.
Isaiah 9:6–7

The world longs for peace, yet we have no peace in the world because we have no peace in our hearts. We need a new heart to love God and love other people. We need a new spirit of reconciliation with God and forgiveness toward others.

The Word promises that when the government of this world is on His shoulders, there will be no end to peace. The answer to conflict and war is Jesus. He will give us a right relationship with God that will produce a right relationship with the people around us. The solution to world conflict— and also the conflict in your home, in your life—is God's only Son, the Prince of Peace.

Pray that the world will be reconciled to God through faith in Jesus, and then be reconciled to each other. Go ... tell someone there is an answer to conflict. Tell him or her about the Prince of Peace.

GIVE GOD YOUR ATTENTION

Pay attention, Job, and listen to me;
be silent, and I will speak.
Job 33:31

When I have to drive long distances, I listen to the radio. The more remote the area, the fewer the stations to choose from, and I find myself listening to programs I've never heard before, just because there's nothing else. But as soon as I approach a city, the signals are jammed with one voice on top of another.

Our lives can be like that radio dial, so jammed with signals that even when we tune in to God's voice, it gets drowned out by other voices. If we're to hear Him clearly, we have to have times of quietness.

There are times when I think God is silent, but in reality He's speaking; I'm just not listening.

In Revelation 1:12, John says, "I turned around to see the voice that was speaking to me." God wants to speak to you! Stop what you're doing, turn around, and give Him your attention.

PEACE

The LORD gives strength to his people;
the LORD blesses his people with peace.
Psalm 29:11

A friend of mine tells the story of her son's emergency appendectomy. He'd gone skiing with friends when he was rushed to the hospital with severe pain. He had the surgery miles away from his parents. As she was telling this to her friends, they were sympathetic to how dreadful the emotional turmoil must have been for her. You can imagine how surprised they were when she said, "There wasn't any turmoil. I'd prayed, and I knew God would take care of my son. And He did!"

That's what Scripture means by peace that passes all understanding (see Philippians 4:7 KJV). Just before Jesus concluded His prayer time in the Garden of Gethsemane, "he looked toward heaven and prayed" (John 17:1). Through eyes of faith, He could see His beloved Father—with an expression of loving trust.

Trust Him. Look into His face. He will give you peace!

NO MORE TEARS

You, O LORD, have delivered my soul from death,
my eyes from tears, my feet from stumbling.
Psalm 116:8

In John 14:1–3, Jesus told His disciples, "Do not let your hearts be troubled. Trust in God; trust also in me. In my Father's house are many rooms ... I am going there to prepare a place for you. And if I go and prepare a place for you, I will come back and take you to be with me that you also may be where I am."

In heaven God Himself will wipe the tears from your face. There'll be no more suffering. Everything will be new. No scars on your memories or your heart.

God can take the ugly stains in our lives, those scars that run deep, and transform them into masterpieces of His grace and mercy that will bless others.

It's time for a makeover. Even now God can turn the ugliness of sin into beauty marks. Just come to Him and ask. Surrender your scars to His gentle touch.

KEEP SUNDAY SPECIAL

*In six days the LORD made the heavens and the
earth, the sea, and all that is in them, but he
rested on the seventh day. Therefore the LORD
blessed the Sabbath day and made it holy.*

Exodus 20:11

When God finished creating the earth, He looked around and saw all that He had made, and on the seventh day ... He rested.

Isaiah 58:13–14 says, "If you call the Sabbath a delight and the LORD's holy day honorable, and if you honor it by not going your own way ..., then you will find your joy in the LORD." Is there any reason you can't set aside a day of rest?

Make a list of what you're doing on Sunday: shopping, housework, laundry, yard work, phone calls, email, business appointments, office work. Then make a deliberate decision to do it Monday through Saturday. Reserve Sunday for physical and spiritual refreshment.

Set your heart deep in God. Find your rest in Him. Enjoy inner peace and quiet. Don't miss God's blessing! Keep Sunday special.

GOD IS A GENTLEMAN

I will listen to what God the LORD will say;
he promises peace to his people, his saints.
Psalm 85:8

Perhaps this is one of those times when fear and worry are constant companions …

Maybe you've just said good-bye to a loved one who's serving in the military.

Maybe you're suddenly facing life as a single parent.

Maybe your business is in trouble.

If you're enduring one of these times, ask God to give you a specific promise in His Word, one you can base your faith on.

Before the flood came, God promised Noah that everyone in the ark would be kept alive. Noah's peace rested on his faith in God's promise.

Faith based simply on what you want or feel isn't genuine faith. Hebrews 11:7 says, "By faith Noah, when warned about things not yet seen, in holy fear built an ark to save his family."

God is a Gentleman. He keeps His Word.

GOD IS FAITHFUL

"Have faith in God," Jesus answered. "I tell you the truth,
if anyone says to this mountain, 'Go, throw yourself into
the sea,' and does not doubt in his heart but believes
that what he says will happen, it will be done for him."
Mark 11:22–23

Do you think God's silence in your life means He's forgotten you? Nothing could be further from the truth! The Bible says God has engraved your name on the palms of His hands (Isaiah 49:16). You're in God's heart and on His mind every moment. He's fully informed of your circumstances and will deliver you when He knows the time is right.

Just as He was faithful to preserve Joseph through thirteen years of slavery in Egypt ... just as He was faithful to preserve Daniel in the lions' den ... just as He was faithful to preserve the baby Moses floating on the Nile—God will be faithful to you!

Why? Because God *is* faithful! It's who He is! So don't be afraid. He cannot be less than Himself. Have faith in God!

ALWAYS ON TIME

I wait for you, O LORD; you will answer, O Lord my God.
Psalm 38:15

I hate to wait. It's so hard, especially when I'm waiting on the Lord. Sometimes He seems to be *soooo* slow. But I've learned over the years—and sometimes still forget!—that waiting is an essential part of spiritual discipline. In fact, it can be the ultimate test of our faith.

In Psalm 27:14, David says, "Wait for the LORD; be strong and take heart and wait for the LORD." If you wait on God, you will be blessed.

But we get impatient and take things into our own hands, and that's where we get into trouble. Like Abraham, who waited ten years for a son and couldn't wait any longer—and so had Ishmael. We are still paying the price for his impatience.

Are you waiting on God for something? Keep waiting! God is always on time.

HE WAITS PATIENTLY

"Give ear and come to me; hear me, that your soul may live."
Isaiah 55:3

There's nothing more frustrating than having to be somewhere quickly and discovering you're out of gas—literally running on empty!

It's true of our emotional and spiritual life as well. Your personal gauge points to empty, and you wonder, *Where's the happiness? The satisfaction? The joy?*

As Jesus returned to Galilee, John 4:4 says, "he had to go through Samaria." There was only one reason to take a route through that place of outcasts. It was because He had a divine appointment with one person whose life was running on empty.

The Bible says, "Jesus, tired as he was from the journey, sat down by the well" (John 4:6). Bone weary, He was waiting to meet with one person. And still today, Jesus waits patiently to meet with anyone who'll come to Him.

Your divine appointment with Jesus may be this very moment. Jesus is right here, right now. Wanting to meet with you. Don't keep Him waiting.

HEAR HIS VOICE

Love the LORD your God, listen to his
voice, and hold fast to him.
Deuteronomy 30:20

H as someone said to you, "God would never want you to stay in your miserable marriage—He wants you to be happy"? Or, "If you had more faith, you'd be healed"? Words like that can put us in a tailspin and cause spiritual doubt, even when made by sincere friends.

Learning to recognize the voice of God is critical for your own peace of mind, but also for developing a personal relationship with God—and for living a life pleasing to Him.

Make sure the voice you follow is authentically biblical. Paul warned the church in Galatians 1:7, "Evidently some people are throwing you into confusion and are trying to pervert the gospel of Christ."

Jesus said in John 10:3–4 that He "calls his own sheep by name and leads them out.... His sheep follow him because they know his voice." Learn to discern and recognize your Shepherd's voice.

HOW TO HANDLE A CRISIS

You will keep in perfect peace him whose mind
is steadfast, because he trusts in you.
Isaiah 26:3

The reason a crisis *is* a crisis is because it usually catches us by surprise. To be prepared for the unexpected, we need to spend time every day in prayer. That lifetime habit of daily prayer helps us deal with a crisis when it hits because we've spent time in our Father's presence.

When you neglect prayer, you deprive yourself of the spiritual strength you need to endure and overcome it. It's totally possible to handle a crisis with confidence when you've spent time with your heavenly Father in prayer.

If you want the kind of peace that the Bible says passes all understanding, especially when you are confronting a crisis or have come under enormous pressure, listen to me: you need the spiritual strength and refreshment that only comes from spending time in prayer. Pray. Trust Him. And experience His perfect peace.

PEACE IN GOD'S PRESENCE

"Do not let your hearts be troubled.
Trust in God; trust also in me."
John 14:1

The antidote to fear is faith. When you toss and turn in the middle of the night, worried and fearful over something that's going on in your life or the life of someone you love, be comforted and calmed as you think on who God is. Make a mental list of His attributes. Alphabetize the list to help you focus on and remember who He is.

He is bigger than your fears because He's able, benevolent, compassionate, dependable, eternal, faithful, good, and on and on.

Jesus' statement "Do not let your heart be troubled" is not a suggestion. It's a command that you and I are to obey. Our obedience begins with a choice to stop being afraid, followed by a decision to start trusting God. He's the God of gods, who's made Himself visible and knowable and approachable through Jesus Christ. Just trust Him! *Trust Him!*

WHEN YOU FEEL AFRAID

The LORD appeared to him and said, "I am
the God of your father Abraham. Do not be
afraid, for I am with you; I will bless you."
Genesis 26:24

I had a dear young friend who began experiencing dreadful panic attacks. On the advice of friends, she began seeing a psychiatrist, who walked her through a simple exercise of listing everything she was afraid of. When she finished her list, her fears so dominated her thinking, she could no longer even function.

It can be helpful to pinpoint the source of worries and fears, but to dwell on them may put you into a downward spiral. Next time you feel afraid, make up your own list—not of your fears but of the characteristics of God. Find a Scripture verse or passage to substantiate each one of those characteristics as you reconsider your situation in light of who God is. Then claim God's promise: "Do not be afraid, for I am with you."

The secret to peace lies in your focus!

BE AN EXAMPLE

God did not give us a spirit of timidity, but a spirit
of power, of love and of self-discipline.
2 Timothy 1:7

The apostle Paul taught Timothy, his "beloved child," three things we should be teaching our children today:

1. Don't be afraid to live for Jesus.
2. Don't be ashamed to live for Jesus.
3. Don't be apathetic in living for Jesus.

Paul reached out in encouragement in 2 Timothy 1:8: "So do not be ashamed to testify about our Lord.... But join with me in suffering for the gospel, by the power of God." And later Paul said to Timothy, "Continue in what you have learned and have become convinced of, because you know those from whom you learned it" (3:14).

Give your children the example of a parent who isn't afraid to live for Christ.

Be courageous.

Be confident.

Be absolutely committed to God's work and God's Word!

Start setting the example now.

WALK BY FAITH

About midnight Paul and Silas were praying
and singing hymns to God, and the other
prisoners were listening to them.
Acts 16:25

As Christians, we say we walk by faith, but do we fully understand what it means?

Jeremiah preached faithfully for more than sixty years without ever having a positive response to his message. In fact, he faced being stoned to death. But he lived by faith!

When the apostle Paul was thrown into prison because he'd preached the gospel of Jesus Christ, he lived by faith. In fact, Paul prayed and sang hymns to God in prison. Can you imagine what those jailers must have thought? I doubt very much that Paul felt like singing. But he had learned to live by faith, not by his feelings.

God commands you and me to exercise our will, to make the deliberate, conscious choice to walk by faith. Start trusting God. Live by faith in Him—and in His Word.

SERIOUS ABOUT GOD'S WORK

*May the favor of the Lord our God rest upon
us; establish the work of our hands for us—
yes, establish the work of our hands.*
Psalm 90:17

God is looking for those who'll take their service to Him seriously. Are you someone God is looking for?

I'm convinced that the time to serve Christ is *now*. The words of Jesus in John 9:4 haunt me continuously: "As long as it is day, we must do the work of him who sent me. Night is coming, when no one can work."

It is most definitely time to get serious about our service to Christ. To be prepared. To be persevering. God doesn't want careless, casual Christians in His service.

In the Old Testament, He whittled down Gideon's army from thirty-two thousand men to three hundred by weeding out those who didn't take service to Him seriously.

Paul gave everything, including his own life, to serve Christ.

Can God take *you* seriously? The night is coming. Work for Him today!

WE FORGIVE OTHERS

"I will forgive their wickedness and will
remember their sins no more."
Jeremiah 31:34

Forgiveness is difficult, especially if you think it's about your feelings.
It isn't. It's about God! We forgive others, not because they deserve it,
but because *He* deserves it. In His agony on the cross, Jesus said, "Father,
forgive them" (Luke 23:34). If Jesus forgave those who nailed Him to the
cross, and if God forgives you and me, how can you withhold your forgiveness from someone else?

If God says, "I forgive you," who are we to say, "Thank You, God, but
I can't forgive someone else—or even myself"? Are your standards higher
than His? More *righteous* than His?

If God says, "I forgive you," the only appropriate response is, "God,
thank You. I don't deserve it, but I accept it. And to express my gratitude
I, in turn, forgive the person who's sinned against me—even if that person
is me."

Make your forgiveness your act of worship.

CUTTING AND PRUNING

"I am the true vine, and my Father is the gardener.
He cuts off every branch in me that bears no
fruit, while every branch that does bear fruit he
prunes so that it will be even more fruitful."
John 15:1–2

As I drove up to my friend's home, I couldn't help but notice how beautifully landscaped his yard was. It was like a page out of a gardening magazine. The grass looked soft and inviting, like a carpet. Flowers were blooming, and everything was beautifully clipped and pruned, obviously by someone who knew what he was doing. The entire scene pointed to attention, skill, and loving care.

As I looked at it, I couldn't help but wonder, *What do people think when they look at the garden of my life? Does it look lovingly cultivated? Or more like an overgrown, weed-infested jungle?*

Jesus said to His disciples in John 15:8, "This is to my Father's glory, that you bear much fruit, showing yourselves to be my disciples."

If you want to have a beautiful life of cultivated discipleship, submit yourself to the cutting and pruning of the master Gardener.

LAY YOUR QUESTIONS DOWN

Jesus said to her, "I am the resurrection and the life. He who
believes in me will live, even though he dies; and whoever
lives and believes in me will never die. Do you believe this?"

John 11:25–26

Have you ever cried out, "God, don't You see my broken heart? *Why* don't You do something? Do You care?"

Or have you ever prayed, "I just don't understand why You allowed that to happen"? And, "God, *why* did You do *that*?"

What are your *why* questions?

Outside her brother's tomb, Martha cried out, "Lord, . . . if you had been here, my brother would not have died" (John 11:21). As Jesus wept with Martha, with her tears on His face, He challenged her to believe. "Your brother will rise again," He said (v. 23).

In other words, "Martha, put your faith in Me. Trust Me when you don't understand why. I have a greater purpose in mind than just healing your brother. I plan to raise him from the dead!" And Jesus did!

Lay your *why* questions at the feet of Jesus and trust Him when you don't understand. Trust Him!

SHOWING IS BETTER THAN TELLING

But if anyone obeys his word, God's love is truly made
complete in him. This is how we know we are in him:
Whoever claims to live in him must walk as Jesus did.
1 John 2:5–6

An old farmer wanted to teach his new farmhand a lesson. He pointed out the stalls where he kept his mules, the feed bins, and the corral where he kept his prize mule. The farmer ducked under the pole fence, walked up to the mule, and stroked its neck.

The young man did the same thing—but approached the mule from behind. The mule kicked out his leg and sent the young man flying across the stall.

"Why didn't you tell me that mule would kick?" he said.

The old farmer waited a second and then said, "Well—showin' is better'n tellin'!"

Often family, friends, and co-workers will watch what we do much more closely than they'll listen to what we say.

Sometimes showing *is* better than telling!

NOT SOMEHOW, BUT VICTORIOUSLY!

> If the LORD delights in a man's way, he makes his steps firm.
> *Psalm 37:23*

I'm sure you've used the expression, "Somehow, we'll make it." Or, "Somehow, it'll all turn out okay."

I'm so glad faith in Jesus isn't a "somehow" kind of faith. Aren't you? God plants you and me in our faith like tender saplings—then grows us up into what Isaiah 61 describes as "oaks of righteousness" (v. 3).

God leads us to endure, not just "somehow," but victoriously. In Psalm 13:5–6, King David wrote his prayer to God: "I trust in your unfailing love; my heart rejoices in your salvation. I will sing to the LORD, for he has been good to me."

When Paul was in prison, beaten and maligned because he'd preached the gospel, guards heard him singing praises to God. Paul had learned to walk by faith, not by his feelings.

It's time to grow up. Make a deliberate, conscious choice to trust in the Lord always. Stop living by your feelings. Start living by faith.

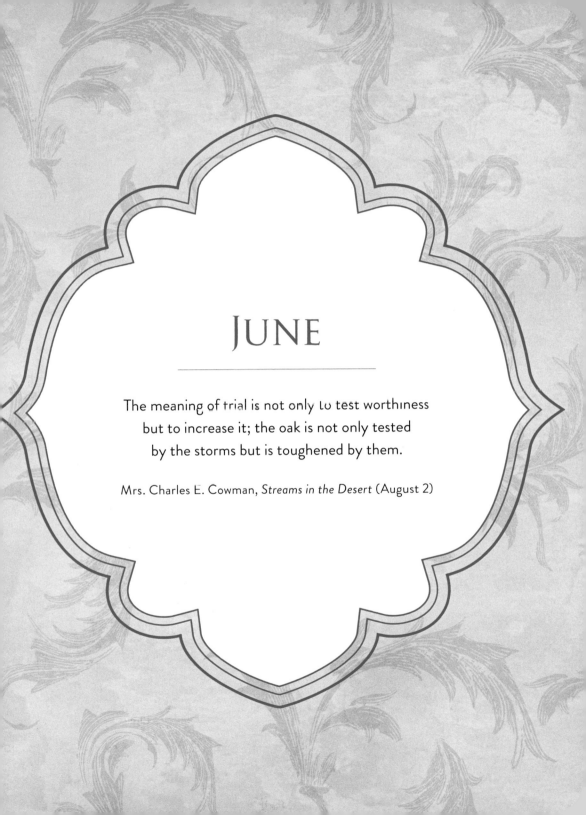

JUNE

The meaning of trial is not only to test worthiness
but to increase it; the oak is not only tested
by the storms but is toughened by them.

Mrs. Charles E. Cowman, *Streams in the Desert* (August 2)

BE INTENTIONAL

Because of the service by which you have proved yourselves,
men will praise God for the obedience that accompanies
your confession of the gospel of Christ, and for your
generosity in sharing with them and with everyone else.
2 Corinthians 9:13

You can't beat athletes for intensity. I spoke to a group of professional women golfers and was impressed by their focus. Everything—their diet, schedule, activities, friendships—revolved around one purpose: being the best golfers they could be.

I shared with them that I have a similar sense of purpose that dictates where I go, how I spend my money, what I say and do. Simply put, God's purpose for my life is to grow increasingly in my personal knowledge of God as I follow Him in a life of faith. And then to make Him known to others.

To work out that purpose requires me to be intentional in the way I spend my time and money. Where I go and what I do and who I'm with.

Be an intentional follower of Jesus!

ABSOLUTE TRUTH

You will go on before the Lord to prepare the
way for him, to give his people the knowledge of
salvation through the forgiveness of their sins,
because of the tender mercy of our God.
Luke 1:76–78

The buzzword of our time is *pluralism*, the idea that there's truth in almost everything and no one thing can make a claim of absolute truth over the other.

Religious pluralism says that if you're truly loving, you'll tolerate the false and compromise. In other words, let's not offend anyone. After all, our religious beliefs are personal.

But Jesus defied any kind of pluralism when He proclaimed in John 14:6, "No one comes to the Father except through me." Think about it. You may be Asian, Spanish, Muslim, or Jewish—it makes no difference. Jesus Christ is the answer to peace in the world, to a right relationship with God, to a heavenly home for every man and woman. He is the Way. There is no other.

Religions and peoples have some truth; of course they do. But only Jesus Christ is *the* truth for everyone.

If there were another way to God, don't you think He would have found it?

COURAGE TO STAND ALONE

He ... will greatly honor those who acknowledge him.
Daniel 11:39

D anny Wuerffel was quarterback for the University of Florida when he was named *Playboy* magazine's 1996 National Scholar Athlete of the Year. It was a very prestigious award, and Danny was invited to receive it at an exclusive resort. But he politely refused!

Danny was publicly criticized while another athlete received the honor. That took strength. Strength that came from Danny talking to God and reading his Bible. It came from listening to God and from caring more about what God thinks than what others think.

Deuteronomy 30:20 says, "Love the LORD your God, listen to his voice, and hold fast to him." *Hold fast!* It's key to giving you the courage to endure criticism and stand fast instead of going along with something that doesn't honor God.

At the end of the 1996 football season, Danny was given the coveted Heisman Trophy for best college football player of the year. Danny honored God—and God honored Danny. Will you be one whom God honors because you've had the courage to stand alone?

COMMUNICATING WITH GOD

The LORD would speak to Moses face to
face, as a man speaks with his friend.
Exodus 33:11

Communication is an important key to a relationship. Yet how often we neglect doing what is necessary to develop it.

If one person does all the talking but never listens, the relationship goes nowhere. Relationships require communication, which requires talking and listening. Our relationship with God is no exception. We need to talk to Him in prayer. But to *communicate* with Him, we can't do *all* the talking. We also need to listen to what He has to say as we read our Bibles.

When God spoke to Abraham, He revealed what was on His mind (see Genesis 18:20–33).

In response, Abraham questioned God, wanting to understand. God answered. Then Abraham asked another question. More than half a dozen times, there was a back-and-forth dialogue. Abraham *communicated* with God. As a result of his earnest, persistent prayer, his nephew, Lot, was saved from judgment.

Who would be saved if you would learn to communicate with God?

WILLING TO BE SERVED

[Jesus] came to Simon Peter, who said to him,
"Lord, are you going to wash my feet?"
John 13:6

When Peter asked Jesus, "Lord, are you going to wash my feet?" he revealed an attitude so typical of you and me today: pride! It can be a serious wound to our pride, not only to serve, but to be served.

For years I taught a Bible study class of five hundred women. I was overwhelmed with preparing for the class and being a wife and a mom to three small children. So the women divided themselves into pairs to provide an entire dinner for my family on the weeknight of the class. I needed their help and was genuinely touched by their loving support, *but* ... their kind gesture seemed to represent my failure to provide for my family and myself.

Eventually, with shame, I realized my resistance was rooted in pride.

God clearly commands you and me, "Humble yourselves" (1 Peter 5:6). It's important that we be willing to serve. But we also need to be willing to *be served* by others!

CLIP, CLIP

"This is to my Father's glory, that you bear much
fruit, showing yourselves to be my disciples."
John 15:8

While *cutting* is drastic and encourages new growth, *clipping* is used to control and shape the growth of a plant. It encourages fruitfulness by concentrating the energy of the vine into the fruitful areas of the branch. A wise gardener clips even a fruitful branch. Jesus described the process in John 15:2: "Every branch that does bear fruit he prunes so that it will be even more fruitful."

I know that "clip, clip" very well!

When I pray for patience and God puts me with a very demanding person—clip!

When I pray for strength and I'm scheduled for surgery—clip!

When I pray for faith and my son is diagnosed with cancer—clip!

Are you resisting the Gardener's clip? Read again the verse at the top of the page and remember: your purpose, and mine, is to bring glory to God!

A PROMISED REWARD

"Your Father, who sees what is done
in secret, will reward you."
Matthew 6:4

Our children were expected to do their share of housework. But when we asked them to do even more, we'd add a little motivation with a cash reward! It was amazing to see the difference the promised reward made—in their attitude and in the quality of their work. They were much more pleasant and much more conscientious!

The same is true in your Christian life. The promise of a reward adds eagerness and energy. As a result, our attitudes go from "I *have* to do this" to "I *want* to do this."

Let the reward of God's pleasure motivate you. Let the reward of a crown to lay at His feet give you energy to serve Him with joy.

WHAT A PLEASURE!

Dear children, let us not love with words or tongue
but with actions and in truth. This then is how
we know that we belong to the truth, and how
we set our hearts at rest in his presence.
1 John 3:18–19

How are you serving the Lord in your home? In your office? At church? In the community? Perhaps more important, what's your attitude when you serve Him?

John 13:1–30 gives at least four characteristics of an attitude of service if you're following the example of the Lord.

We're to serve willingly—when it's not convenient or even when our service isn't appreciated.

We're to serve humbly. What job are you too proud to do?

We're to serve obediently. What is your motivation for service?

And we're to serve sincerely.

Psalm 103:20–21 says, "Praise the LORD, you his angels, … who obey his word … , you his servants who do his will." What a pleasure to do God's pleasure! The greatest joy you'll experience on earth, other than worshiping our Lord, is the joy of working for Him—willingly, humbly, obediently.

SALTY SAINTS

"You are the salt of the earth. But if the salt loses its
saltiness, how can it be made salty again? It is no longer good
for anything, except to be thrown out and trampled by men."
Matthew 5:13

S alt can be used in food as a preservative, but it can also make people thirsty and food tasty. Jesus said those who believe in Him are the salt of the earth; our function is to make others hungry and thirsty for Him.

Are you losing your saltiness? Today it's easy to become so saturated in selfishness and materialism, so engrossed by entertainment and politics, so anesthetized by religion and tradition, that we're in danger of losing the uniqueness of who we are in Christ. As a result our "salt" no longer makes people "thirsty" for Jesus or the things of God "tasty."

When that happens, we desperately need to recharge our saltiness by renewing our personal knowledge of God, our passionate love for Christ, our practical devotion to the Holy Spirit, and our purposeful commitment to the gospel so that once again, we are salty believers.

Be the salty saint that you are!

SPEAK BOLDLY

Then Paul and Barnabas answered them boldly:
"We had to speak the word of God to you."
Acts 13:46

Most of us want to share our testimony of what Jesus has done in our lives, but we're just too afraid! So we're silent. We back off, opting instead for a "lifestyle" kind of evangelism in the hope that our actions speak louder than words.

Jesus said in Revelation 2:10, "Do not be afraid." He wants us to take God's peace, share our testimony, and leave the consequences to Him.

When Queen Esther was challenged to take a stand against Haman's plotted holocaust of the Jews, she said, "I will go to the king, even though it is against the law. And if I perish, I perish" (Esther 4:16). In the end, she did not perish. The Jews to this day celebrate the Feast of Purim to commemorate her courage and the deliverance of God's people that was the result of it.

Take a stand! Speak out! Then leave the consequences to God.

MORE IN THE END

If [his gift] is encouraging, let him encourage; if it
is contributing to the needs of others, let him give
generously; if it is leadership, let him govern diligently;
if it is showing mercy, let him do it cheerfully.

Romans 12:8

Jesus will more than meet your needs ... as you meet the needs of others.

In John 6:12, after five thousand people had been fed, Jesus said to His disciples, "Gather the pieces that are left over. Let nothing be wasted." Was Jesus just being environmentally friendly? Or was He giving them a final lesson?

When they'd gathered all the leftovers, they filled twelve baskets! *Twelve.* Get the connection? There's no coincidence or mistake that there was obviously one basket of bread for each of the twelve disciples.

Are you afraid that if Jesus asks you to reach out to help others and you give Jesus everything, you'll somehow come up short? That you'll end up with *less*?

Listen to me: you can't outgive God. Remember that the disciples had more in the end than they had in the beginning.

Give God all you have—and you will end up with more!

DO YOU CARE?

Jesus said to Simon Peter, "Simon son of John,
do you truly love me more than these?"
"Yes, Lord," he said, "you know that I love you."
Jesus said, "Feed my lambs."
John 21:15

When we care about our weight, we go on a diet.

When we care about our shape, we begin an exercise program.

When we care about national policy, we vote.

In other words, when we care about something or someone, we do something about it! After Jesus asked Peter three times if he loved Him, He then said, "Feed my lambs.... Feed my sheep" (John 21:15–17).

What does it mean to "feed" Jesus' lambs? Lambs are little sheep ... children. We "feed" His children by teaching them the simple stories and truth of God's Word.

Jesus said, "Let the little children come to me, and do not hinder them, for the kingdom of God belongs to such as these" (Luke 18:16). We hinder children from coming to Jesus by not giving them God's Word.

Do you truly love Jesus? Do you care about Him? If you do, then start feeding His lambs today!

JUST DO IT SCARED!

> "When the Counselor comes, whom I will send to
> you from the Father, the Spirit of truth who goes
> out from the Father, he will testify about me."
> *John 15:26*

When have you spoken up for Jesus? When have you told someone about Jesus who doesn't know Him?

I understand how fearful you might be. Maybe you're afraid your neighbor will never speak to you again. Or your friends will laugh. Or you're fearful you'll lose popularity or a promotion or a position or prestige. You could probably name any number of things that could keep you from being a witness for Christ.

Jesus understands all your fears. That's why He's sent you and me the Holy Spirit. When we speak, the Holy Spirit not only gives us the words—He makes those words powerful to make a difference in the hearers.

So ... just do it scared!

A Heart for the Gospel

[Jesus] said, "I must preach the good news of the kingdom of
God to the other towns also, because that is why I was sent."
Luke 4:43

Someone has said that the *world* is the ground between your own two feet! Remember this when you consider that the Bible says, "Go into all the world and preach the gospel" (Mark 16:15 NJKV). That means you and me.

At the conclusion of a recent conference where I'd been the speaker and had prayed that our entire ministry would be worth it, a woman came up to me to say, "Anne, your ministry is worth it! I accepted Christ." She shared that during our meetings in another city, she had prayed to receive Christ. She was coming now to learn how to read, study, and teach the Scriptures so she might pass on God's Word to someone else.

Would you ask God to give you a heart for the gospel? Then would you be obedient to the command of our Lord to go into your world and tell others about Jesus? Take the first step now.

DON'T HIDE THE LIGHT

The LORD is my light and my salvation—
whom shall I fear? The LORD is the stronghold
of my life—of whom shall I be afraid?
Psalm 27:1

Not long ago, I sat watching the sun come up over Santorini, a beautiful little Greek town on the rim of a volcano. The cluster of white houses draped over the rim of the volcano reflected the early-morning sun. The setting reminded me of what Jesus said to His disciples, as recorded in Matthew 5:14–15: "You are the light of the world. A city on a hill cannot be hidden. Neither do people light a lamp and put it under a bowl. Instead they put it on its stand, and it gives light to everyone in the house."

Don't be intimidated into hiding your light! Ask God to use your life to bring clarity and brightness to family, friends, and neighbors, to the people you work with and go to school with, so all might "see your good deeds and praise your Father in heaven" (Matthew 5:16).

If all people knew of Jesus was what they see in your life, how much would they know? Don't hide the light. Let it shine!

WE HAVE WORK TO DO

*"I have brought you glory on earth by
completing the work you gave me to do."*
John 17:4

G od has work for us to do, just as He gave His Son work while He was
on earth.

Our work is like the rim of a wheel with several spokes connected to the
hub as channels. The hub is our focus, and it's to be centered on fulfilling
God's purpose for our lives.

One spoke may be to be a godly husband, helping your wife fulfill God's
purpose for her life. Another spoke might be to be a godly mother, raising
children to fulfill God's purpose for their lives. Or a godly grandparent, or
to study and teach God's Word in such a way that others are compelled to
seek and fulfill God's purpose for their lives.

If you and I are able to finish God's work, it won't be by accident. We
will need to stay focused with singleness of heart and mind on God as
the center of our lives and let ourselves be a channel of His love to those
around us.

Finish the work God has given you to do!

SMALL THINGS

"Though it is the smallest of all your seeds, yet when it
grows, it is the largest of garden plants and becomes a tree,
so that the birds of the air come and perch in its branches."
Matthew 13:32

Two thousand years ago, a tiny handful of women changed the world.
When Paul received a vision calling him to Europe, he ended up
at Philippi. There he found no synagogue, no body of believers. On the
Sabbath he went to the river where a group of women had gathered with a
prominent businesswoman named Lydia. She invited Paul to her home so
she and the others could hear the gospel. From that tiny handful of women,
the church was born in Philippi.

Recently I sat with others on a riverbank in Philippi. We took
Communion and remembered Jesus. We remembered that small group of
women and a church that spread across Europe and into the world, including
what is today America.

The prophet Zechariah asked, "Who despises the day of small things?"
(4:10). What opportunity have you ignored or missed or refused to take
because it seemed so small? Remember the Philippian church. Don't despise
small things.

STRONGER CONVICTIONS

And you also were included in Christ when you heard
the word of truth, the gospel of your salvation.
Ephesians 1:13

I'm basically shy. So when I was asked by an interviewer if my boldness for my faith was hereditary, I thought a moment and said, "I'm bold because I'm convinced what I say about Jesus is the truth."

Maybe you and I don't need more courage. Maybe we need stronger convictions. When you feel deeply about something, you're compelled to open your mouth and speak up.

In John 15:27, Jesus said to His disciples, "You also must testify, for you have been with me from the beginning." When Peter and John said boldly, "Salvation is found in no one else" except in Jesus, the authorities could hardly believe their ears. They realized Peter and John were unschooled, ordinary men, and were astonished. They took note that these men had been with Jesus (Acts 4:12–13).

Fill your heart with Jesus. Then let His words come out on your lips!

SEE PEOPLE AS GOD SEES THEM

When he saw the crowds, he had compassion
on them, because they were harassed and
helpless, like sheep without a shepherd.
Matthew 9:36

How do you see people—including those who interrupt your family time?

Or an increasingly senile parent who tries your patience?

Or neighbors who drop by when it's not convenient?

Or just a lonely friend who calls you and talks too long?

I've had to ask God to help me see people through His eyes. If we're going to meet the needs of others, we must not view people as interruptions. When the disciples saw Jesus being interrupted—bothered by children who'd gathered—they began shooing them away. But Jesus said no (and quite emphatically, I might add). "Let the little children come to me," He told them (Matthew 19:14).

We must be willing to see people from God's perspective. And we must be willing to give up some of our own time to help meet their needs. Jesus saw people as God saw them, and He calls on us to do the same.

FEED THE LAMBS

"Whoever welcomes one of these little children in
my name welcomes me; and whoever welcomes me
does not welcome me but the one who sent me."
Mark 9:37

What lambs come to mind when you think about Jesus' instruction to Simon Peter in John 21:15: "[If you] love me . . . feed my lambs"?

Maybe they're the lambs you carpool to the soccer game. Or the students who drop by with your teenager after class. Or the children in the neighborhood who play with your children.

A lovely woman shared how she got involved in feeding "lambs." Her two daughters rode the school bus that stopped right in front of their house. Every morning a dozen children gathered there. One morning it was pouring rain, so she invited the children to wait inside her front door. While they waited, she read a Bible verse and prayed for them. Every morning, from then on, the children gathered at her front door to hear a Bible verse.

Do you love Jesus? Then feed His lambs!

STONES OF REMEMBRANCE

Each of you is to take up a stone on his shoulder ... to serve
as a sign among you. In the future, when your children ask
you, "What do these stones mean?" tell them. ... These
stones are to be a memorial to the people of Israel forever.

Joshua 4:5–7

What evidence of God's power is there in your life? Is there enough evidence so that others ask you for an explanation?

After wandering in the wilderness for forty years, the Israelites experienced the power of God to roll back the Jordan River, enabling them to cross over and take possession of the promised land. Then they built a memorial of stones as evidence of what God had done for them. In Joshua 4:21–22, 24, God said, "In the future when your descendants ask ..., 'What do these stones mean?' tell them ... so that all the peoples of the earth might know the hand of the LORD is powerful and so that you might always fear the LORD your God."

What are your stones of remembrance? Keep a journal of your thoughts, your prayers. Write a letter. Leave some personal word of testimony so that your children and grandchildren will know God's power in your life. And they will be encouraged to collect and build their own stones of remembrance for the generation that follows theirs.

It's the Holy Spirit's Job

> "When he comes, he will convict the world of guilt in
> regard to sin and righteousness and judgment."
> *John 16:8*

How do we convince someone today that Jesus, who lived two thousand years ago, is relevant today? How do we convince a sinner of his or her sin? How do we convince others of the need to get right with God? We can't do it! But the Holy Spirit of God can!

What impossible tasks these would be without the Holy Spirit. My wise mother said to me years ago, "Anne, it's your job to make your husband happy, and it's the Holy Spirit's job to make him good."

Before you open your mouth to speak for Christ, before you ever begin your day to live for Christ—pray! Pray that the Holy Spirit will take what you give out, what you live out, and use it to convict others of their need to be right with God.

SET THE CAPTIVES FREE

To each one of us grace has been given as Christ
apportioned it. This is why it says: "When he ascended on
high, he led captives in his train and gave gifts to men."
Ephesians 4:7–8

Instead of complaining, wringing our hands, and blaming and criticizing others when the enemy attacks, what would happen if we separated ourselves from the crowd and turned to God in prayer?

What would happen if we didn't rely on programs or techniques but relied instead on God's power to gain His perspective, to recognize His call to get involved, and then to pursue those held captive by the enemy? By their own sin? By their appetites and desires? By their habits and addictions?

Abraham, living under the oak trees of Mamre, was separated from the world around him when he received the news that his nephew Lot had been taken captive. He then pursued and overcame the enemy, setting Lot free. Psalm 20:7 says, "Some trust in chariots and some in horses, but we trust in the name of the LORD our God."

Pray. Then trust in God to give you victory as you go into your world to set the captives free.

THE HOPE OF HEAVEN

Whom have I in heaven but you? And earth
has nothing I desire besides you.
Psalm 73:25

The telephone rang. My friend was calling—moments after her son was born with a deadly disease.

Like the mother of any newborn, she described how beautiful her baby was, and I asked her what she and her husband had named this little boy who would only be theirs for a short while before Jesus would take him to His Father's house.

She hesitated for the briefest moment, then said, "I think we're going to name him Gabriel. He's our little messenger from God."

I prayed, "Thank You, dear God, for the message in Your Word—Your goodness, faithfulness, and righteousness; Your loving-kindness and hope! And thank You for Your precious little messenger Gabriel. Give him a loud voice to proclaim the glory of who You truly are!"

God has given you the hope of heaven in your grief, in your trials. Praise Him for the hope of heaven!

READY TO SETTLE YOUR ACCOUNT

So then, each of us will give an account of himself to God.
Romans 14:12

It seems like the entire world is in chaos. Evil prevails. But there will come a time when wrong is set right!

I'm reminded of a story about an old farmer whose field bordered his neighbor's. On the Lord's Day, the old farmer never worked, but his neighbor always did. The farmer worked hard, but the loss of time cost him. In the end, his fall harvest wasn't as profitable as his neighbor's. The neighbor pointed this out to the old farmer and said, "God seems to bless me even though I haven't honored the Lord's Day."

To which the old farmer replied, "God doesn't settle all of His accounts in October!"

There will be an accounting—if not today, then tomorrow. Judgment is coming. Because God is just. Be sure you are ready today to settle your account tomorrow.

A Spring of Water

"Whoever drinks the water I give him will never
thirst. Indeed, the water I give him will become in
him a spring of water welling up to eternal life."
John 4:14

As Jesus watched the Samaritan woman come to the well to draw water, He knew her heart was empty, without love or self-worth or meaning or happiness. He gently but pointedly said to her, "Everyone who drinks this water will be thirsty again" (John 4:13).

Can you imagine her surprise? The woman thought He meant the water in Jacob's well, but Jesus was speaking to her heart.

If you're looking for satisfaction from the wells of pleasure, popularity, position, prestige, money, fame, even religion, you'll soon be thirsty again. The world can give you meaning and pleasure—temporarily. But you're wasting your time. It'll eventually leave you wondering, *Is that all there is?*

Jesus tells us to drink the water He gives us, and we will never thirst. The Living Water is Jesus. He will be "a spring of water welling up to eternal life." Drink deeply today.

BIG THINGS AND SMALL THINGS

In the beginning God created the heavens and the earth.
Genesis 1:1

The very first verse of the Bible tells us God, as Creator, is active in big ways, like creating the heavens!

What big thing are you confronting? A big decision? A commitment? Responsibility? A big problem?

The very first verse of the Bible tells us also that God is active in small things. He created the earth with its chemical elements, molecules, genes, and atoms—things so small they cannot be seen by the naked eye.

What do you think is too small for God to notice? A small tear? A small hurt feeling? A small deed? A small insult? A small worry that's robbing you of your joy?

God is actively involved in big things and small things. Listen to me: trust the details of your life to the Creator of the heavens and the earth.

SAFE IN ETERNITY

"These commandments that I give you today are to be
upon your hearts. Impress them on your children. Talk
about them when you sit at home and when you walk
along the road, when you lie down and when you get up."
Deuteronomy 6:6–7

I'm sure that you, as a responsible parent, do everything you can to ensure your children's safety. But what are you doing to ensure your children will be safe in eternity?

It's your responsibility and privilege to tell your children about God, about their own sin, about their need to claim Jesus Christ as Savior so their sins will be washed away. And about heaven and how to get there.

God promises in His Word that when we place our faith in Jesus Christ as Savior, we will not perish but have everlasting life—a life lived with God and His family in heaven. He instructs us to impress this promise upon our children.

Pray for your children, your grandchildren, your nieces and nephews. Ask God to work on behalf of the children. Then go! Tell a child today how he or she can be safe forever.

HEAVEN IS GOD'S HOME—AND YOURS!

*There will be no more death or mourning or crying or
pain, for the old order of things has passed away.*
Revelation 21:4

If you live in an older home, like I do, you're dealing with stains and cracks and constant repairs. When I visit friends in their brand-new homes, I look longingly at the unmarked woodwork and painted walls, the fresh, unstained carpet. It's all fresh.

Our planet is thousands of years old—maybe even millions. And it's showing signs of age. But it wasn't created to last forever. A new heaven and a new earth are being prepared!

In Revelation, John gives us a vision of heaven's perfection. It's perfect because God is there. He says you and I "will be his people" there. In heaven, God Himself will be with us and be our God (Revelation 21:3).

Heaven is God's home. Praise God, it's our home too! It's the home of our dreams.

BUILT TO LAST

The wall of the city had twelve foundations, and on them
were the names of the twelve apostles of the Lamb.
Revelation 21:14

Fires and floods are devastating. In minutes an entire neighborhood of homes can be lost. How many times have we sat transfixed by images of total destruction on our TV or computer screens? Everything gone. All that's left is rubble.

In contrast, how reassuring it is to know that if you're a child of God, you have a home built to last, not just for a lifetime, but forever! The apostle John, describing the vision of heaven God gave him, said the wall of that home has twelve foundations and the foundations are decorated with every kind of precious stone. Twelve foundations! So heaven is not only spectacular in its beauty—it's unshakable. Permanent!

Today we live in a very unstable world. We can never be sure of the future for ourselves or for the next generation. But as Christians we can be certain and sure of absolute, total future stability. Heaven is built to last!

JULY

God does not comfort us to make us
comfortable, but to make us comforters.

Mrs. Charles E. Cowman, *Streams in the Desert* (January 11)

THE HOME OF YOUR DREAMS

I saw the Holy City, the new Jerusalem, coming
down out of heaven from God, prepared as a
bride beautifully dressed for her husband.
Revelation 21:2

Anna, just twelve years old, lives in foster care—abandoned by her mother and abused by her father. Recently she was told that she was no longer welcome in her foster home. Those in charge told her they'd decided to keep her brother but not her.

How devastating to this little one. Her dreams of a family and home were totally shattered.

Have your dreams of a home been shattered too? Have the dreams of a place where you're accepted, encouraged, challenged, forgiven, understood, and comforted been destroyed? Jesus promised in John 14:2, "In my Father's house are many rooms... I am going there to prepare a place for you."

There's hope! A heavenly home is being prepared for you.

One day you will live in the home of your dreams!

GET TO WORK

So the wall was completed ... in fifty-two days. When all our
enemies heard about this, all the surrounding nations were
afraid and lost their self-confidence, because they realized
that this work had been done with the help of our God.

Nehemiah 6:15–16

God has built in us the capacity for tremendous satisfaction in work.
Not only in finishing the work but in doing it well. One reason why
unemployment is so devastating is that when you're out of work, you're
denied the satisfaction work can bring. So don't be afraid of hard work. And
don't quit a job before it's finished, because it seems too hard or because
you lose interest or because you get a better offer somewhere else.

Genesis 1 and 2 speak about God's work of creation: "God saw all that
he had made, and it was very good.... God had finished the work he had
been doing; so on the seventh day he rested" (1:31; 2:2). The completed
work not only brought Him satisfaction; it also brought Him glory. When
you quit a job before you're finished, you miss out on the satisfaction that
comes with the completion and rob God of His glory.

Whatever work you are doing, don't quit. Get to work. Finish the job
God has called you to do. Enjoy the satisfaction of a job well done! Then
give God the glory!

TITLE OR TESTIMONY?

We know that we live in him and he in us, because he has
given us of his Spirit. And we have seen and testify that
the Father has sent his Son to be the Savior of the world.

1 John 4:13–14

Do you have a title—or a testimony?

Pharaoh was the king of Egypt. He had the title. In contrast is the Old Testament account of Moses. He had the testimony.

King Nebuchadnezzar, as the Babylonian emperor, had the title, but Shadrach, Meshach, and Abednego had the testimony of surviving the fiery furnace unsinged.

Darius, king of Persia, had the title, but it was Daniel who "praised the God of heaven," testifying to God's power to shut the lions' mouths (Daniel 2:19).

King Herod had the title. But John the Baptist had the testimony.

I wonder. What will be remembered about *you*? Your title? Or your testimony about Jesus?

GOD'S STATUE OF LIBERTY

"So if the Son sets you free, you will be free indeed."
John 8:36

All over the country, today is a day for picnics and fireworks. For parades and marching bands. A celebration of our independence—our freedom!

Second Corinthians 3:17 speaks of an even *greater* freedom: the one we have in Christ. It says, "Now the Lord is the Spirit, and where the Spirit of the Lord is, there is freedom." That freedom is the freedom from the penalty of sin, freedom from the power of sin, freedom from shame and guilt. Freedom from fear of death. Freedom from the devil's grip. Freedom from the grave!

Praise God. Through the cross, God's Statue of Liberty, we are given genuine, lasting, ultimate freedom. We are truly free at last!

IT'S TIME TO GO

How, then, can they call on the one they have not
believed in? And how can they believe in the one
of whom they have not heard? And how can they
hear without someone preaching to them?
Romans 10:14

We're blessed to have so many Bible studies offered in our churches, homes, dorms, and at the office. Bookstore shelves are filled with studies for every conceivable group of people. But I wonder if we are more comfortable studying *about* the Bible than we are in actually *doing* what it says.

Mary Magdalene watched as Jesus was crucified. She'd seen Him die, and she'd seen Him buried. But the Bible says three days later, on the Sunday morning following the crucifixion, she encountered the risen Christ, and in the thrill of that moment, she clung to Him. Jesus said to her, "Do not hold on to me.... Go instead ... and tell ..." (John 20:17). He was commissioning Mary to tell others about Him.

Could it be that the Lord is telling you and me to stop holding on to our Bible studies and Christian groups? The time has come to do something: go and tell others about Jesus!

THE PIECES WILL FIT!

I meditate on your precepts and consider your ways. I
delight in your decrees; I will not neglect your word.
Psalm 119:15–16

When I was little, my grandmother entertained me by opening a box containing hundreds of little funny-shaped pieces of cardboard. A jigsaw puzzle! Putting them together seemed impossible until my grandmother said, "Anne, make sure the color pictures on the puzzle pieces are facing up."

Then I'd look at the cover of the box and try to put the pieces together to match the picture.

In some ways, the Bible is like that jigsaw puzzle. It can seem like bits and pieces with no meaning in themselves. That's why we need the Holy Spirit. When Jesus was walking with His disciples, He "explained to them what was said in all the Scriptures concerning himself" (Luke 24:27). And in John 16:13, Jesus said the Holy Spirit would "guide you into all truth."

He turns over the puzzle pieces one by one—until they come together and we see Jesus!

As you read your Bible, ask the Holy Spirit for guidance. The pieces will fit together!

ASK YOUR QUESTIONS

I trust in your unfailing love; my heart
rejoices in your salvation.
Psalm 13:5

Jesus is never offended by your confusion—or your questions. He knows exactly what you're feeling, and He takes the initiative to help you understand. You simply have to trust Him to know best.

For most of us, that's never easy! You have to trust His silences, respect His mysteries, and wait for His answers. Trust Jesus each and every time, in every situation:

When you pray for the healing of someone you love, and she dies.

When you pray for reconciliation, and you're handed divorce papers.

When you pray for a promotion, and you get laid off.

Trust Him.

We serve a sovereign, living Lord, whose ways are not our ways. Be patient.

Trust Him to know best!

The Sword of the Spirit

Jesus said to him, "Away from me, Satan! For it is written:
'Worship the Lord your God, and serve him only.'"
Matthew 4:10

The Word of God is called the "sword of the Spirit" (Ephesians 6:17). It's your primary offensive weapon against Satan and his minions.

Each time Jesus was attacked by Satan, He countered with, "It is written," or "It is also written," or "For it is written" (Matthew 4). If Jesus used the sword—His Word—as a necessary weapon to defeat the enemy, why do we think we can do without it?

Where is your sword? Is it ready on your mind and in your heart? Or is it tucked away, dusty and unused? Jesus Christ wielded His sword to effectively and victoriously counter every thrust of the enemy. If you follow His example, empowered by His Spirit, you, too, can win this battle!

The Bible says, "The one who is in you is greater than the one who is in the world" (1 John 4:4). You're promised victory in Jesus Christ. So ... pick up your sword!

THE HOLY SPIRIT SPEAKS TO US

All Scripture is God-breathed and is useful for
teaching, rebuking, correcting and training in
righteousness, so that the man of God may be
thoroughly equipped for every good work.
2 Timothy 3:16–17

At a meeting at which I was speaking, after I'd finished my message, a woman came up to me, and the expression on her face was far from friendly. She said, very accusingly, "Who's been telling you about me?"

I didn't know the woman, so I said, "No one."

"Then how did you know about …" and she proceeded to share a very sensitive issue in her life that I'd addressed in my message.

I said to her, "That was the Holy Spirit speaking to you. I know nothing of what you're going through—but He does!"

In John 14:17, Jesus said, the Holy Spirit is the Spirit of truth. Paul told Timothy, "All Scripture is God-breathed," referring to the Spirit-inspired Word of God (2 Timothy 3:16).

God the Holy Spirit speaks to us personally and relevantly and specifically through His Word. What has He been saying to you? Whatever it is, it's the truth!

ARE WE LISTENING?

"Can a mother forget the baby at her breast and
have no compassion on the child she has borne?
Though she may forget, I will not forget you! See, I
have engraved you on the palms of my hands."
Isaiah 49:15–16

I don't know about you, but when I run into someone I've met before and he or she remembers my name, it's a nice feeling. And if that person recalls something personal that we may have shared—that's even better, isn't it?

How much better is the fact that God knows my name! The Shepherd speaks to you and me personally—by name. He knows us inside and out. And when He speaks to us, it's in the language of our own personal lives, sometimes through a verse of Scripture that just jumps off the page.

Again and again God has spoken to me through the pages of my Bible, reassuring me, directing me, expanding my horizons. Psalm 103:13–14 says, "As a father has compassion on his children, so the LORD has compassion on those who fear him; for he knows how we are formed."

God knows us personally. And He speaks to us personally. The question is: are we listening?

TOTALLY DEPLETED?

The law of the LORD is perfect, reviving the soul. The statutes
of the LORD are trustworthy, making wise the simple.
Psalm 19:7

Do you sometimes wake up and realize you're just totally depleted? Physically, emotionally, spiritually?

I certainly do. And when I examine myself, often I find that my dryness of spirit can be traced to three key things:

1. I'm neglecting my Bible study.
2. I'm rushing through my prayer time. I might as well be saying, "Now I lay me down to sleep…." My prayers don't go much deeper than that!
3. I'm not listening to the voice of the Lord because I'm just too busy to be still.

God reveals that He lives "in a high and holy place, but also with him who is contrite and lowly in spirit, to revive the spirit of the lowly and to revive the heart of the contrite" (Isaiah 57:15). So carve out the time you need to spend with the Lord, to confess your sins, to read His Word, to meditate, and to pray. Be revived today.

THE BEST TEACHER

"When he, the Spirit of truth, comes, he will guide you into
all truth. He will not speak on his own; he will speak only
what he hears, and he will tell you what is yet to come."
John 16:13

The Bible is a wonderful book of history and poetry. Anyone can be blessed just by reading it. But as a child of God, you have a unique blessing to go past a surface reading and into its deeper meaning.

Luke 24:45 says Jesus "opened their minds so they could understand the Scriptures." The Holy Spirit gives clarity to the wonderful Book He has inspired. Again and again I have sat at my desk, staring at the Scripture passage I've just read and doodling with my pen because my mind's gone blank. Then I pray and ask the Holy Spirit to unlock the meaning for me, and as I continue to meditate, a thought will come, then another thought, until the passage opens up and I see the treasure that's inside.

The Holy Spirit is the best Teacher. He will guide you into all truth. Be a diligent student.

ARE YOU WILLING?

The eunuch asked Philip, "Tell me, please, who is
the prophet talking about, himself or someone
else?" Then Philip began with that very passage of
Scripture and told him the good news about Jesus.
Acts 8:34–35

P hilip was *willing*! These words describe that most amazing man.
Acts 8 describes how the Spirit of the Lord took Philip from a
revival where hundreds were coming to Christ to a desert road to meet
with one man, an Ethiopian eunuch who desired to know the Scripture. A
man to whom Philip brought the good news of Jesus. They traveled along
the road together, and when they came to some water, Philip baptized the
man right then and there.

Philip was willing to be a deacon, an evangelist; he was willing to serve
in Jerusalem, in Samaria, to lead big meetings. And then he was willing to
go and meet with just one man.

Ultimately Philip was willing to die for his faith, crucified in a similar
way to Jesus. Philip was *willing* to be *faithful* wherever God placed him,
however God wanted to use him.

Ask God to place you where He wants you to be and use you how He
decides is best. Then serve Him faithfully—*willingly*!

DISCOVER WHO GOD IS

I pray also that the eyes of your heart may be enlightened
in order that you may know the hope to which he has
called you, the riches of his glorious inheritance in the
saints, and his incomparably great power for us who believe.
That power is like the working of his mighty strength.
Ephesians 1:18–19

My friend refers to herself as a "fixer." There's nothing she likes better than to mix it up in her friends' lives to solve their problems! She means well, but what she's forgetting is that God sometimes allows us to have problems and be in difficult situations so we can discover His "incomparably great power for us who believe."

What problem are you facing that's bigger than you are? If our lives are always easy, and if all we ever attempt for God is what we know we can handle, how will we ever experience His power and greatness? It's when we're in over our heads, when there's seemingly no way out, that we discover who He truly is.

Do you have a problem? God is the Almighty. He is greater, more powerful than any problem or situation you will ever face. Use this problem as an opportunity to discover who He is!

GOD'S LOVED ONE

How great is the love the Father has lavished on us, that we should be called children of God! And that is what we are!
1 John 3:1

There was a time when I struggled in my marriage relationship. For months I focused on my relationship with my husband. I walked on eggshells all the time trying to be very careful to say the right thing, do the right thing, look or feel or act the right way.

Then God gently impressed on me that my focus was all wrong. I was not to concentrate on my relationship with my husband; instead, I was to concentrate on my relationship with God.

Did you know you're God's special loved one? Why would He love you so much? Well, maybe it's because when you concentrate on Him, you're so saturated in Jesus that when God looks at you, He sees His own precious Son and envelops you in His love—for Jesus' sake.

The Bible says, "God is love" (1 John 4:8, 16). Concentrate on Him. Make knowing God your priority!

HE DESERVES ALL THE GLORY

In a loud voice they sang: "Worthy is the Lamb, who
was slain, to receive power and wealth and wisdom
and strength and honor and glory and praise!"
Revelation 5:12

Corrie ten Boom was interred in a Nazi concentration camp because she hid Jews from the Nazis during World War II. She shared her testimony on many occasions following her release. People would line up to tell her what a blessing she'd been to them. Corrie accepted each compliment as she would a flower. And then, at the end of each day, she offered her "bouquet" to the Lord.

I'm afraid most of us are carrying a wilted bouquet—because we've hung on to it so long, clutching the credit for ourselves. It's been said that we don't seem to mind giving God the glory—as long as we can take a 10 percent commission!

Psalm 71:8 says, "My mouth is filled with *your* praise, declaring your splendor all day long" (italics mine).

To God be the glory—*all of it*!

GOD'S PROMISES

> *Your kingdom is an everlasting kingdom, and your dominion*
> *endures through all generations. The LORD is faithful to*
> *all his promises and loving toward all he has made.*
> *Psalm 145:13*

I love the story of an elderly Korean woman who attended a morning prayer meeting every day with a pair of her husband's shoes. She put them at the front of the church and prayed, "Lord, here are my husband's shoes. I believe one day he'll be here to fill them." One year later, those shoes were filled. Her husband came with her and placed his faith in Jesus Christ.

If you've asked God to change your circumstances, if you've claimed His promise for yourself or for someone you love, how are you demonstrating your faith? Biblical hope isn't based on "hope so." It's rooted in a confidence that, although you haven't yet received what God has promised, you know you will.

What shoes do you have to put before the Lord? The Lord *is* faithful to all His promises!

Face Tomorrow with Joy

Once you were not a people, but now you are
the people of God; once you had not received
mercy, but now you have received mercy.
1 Peter 2:10

How can you and I be faithful to the end? The apostle Peter penned a letter to the early church that exuded passionate love for Christ and exuberant joy in knowing Him—even though Peter's relationship with Christ would cost him his life within the year, as he was tortured and crucified for his faith.

How could Peter be so joyous, so faithful in his commitment to Jesus right up until the end? Peter kept looking up! In 1 Peter 1:21, he says, "Through [Christ] you believe in God, who raised him from the dead and glorified him, and so your faith and hope are in God."

We live in a world shaken by terrorism and disease, floods, famine, and fear. But we can face tomorrow with joy because Christ lives. Our hope and faith are in Him!

PRAISE HIM TODAY

Because of the LORD's great love we are not
consumed, for his compassions never fail. They are
new every morning; great is your faithfulness.
Lamentations 3:22–23

When was the last time you *chose* to praise God, even when you didn't feel like it? Was it when you got the news you'd lost your job or when your child was sick or you'd been diagnosed with cancer?

The prophet Jeremiah knew about making choices, and he knew the secret of victory. He had learned to praise God, even though he'd preached faithfully for sixty-five years without ever having a positive response to his message. He'd been ridiculed and imprisoned. Did Jeremiah feel like praising God? I doubt it! And yet in the book of Lamentations he did just that, praising God for His compassions that are "new every morning" and His great faithfulness.

In Hebrews 13:15, we are reminded, "Through Jesus, therefore, let us continually offer to God a *sacrifice* of praise" (italics mine).

Don't wait until you feel like praising God. Follow the example of the prophet Jeremiah and so many others, and just start praising Him today!

STRONG AND COURAGEOUS

Be strong and courageous. Do not be terrified;
do not be discouraged, for the LORD your
God will be with you wherever you go.
Joshua 1:9

The Israelites had wandered for forty years, going nowhere with God. Then God instructed them, under Joshua's leadership, to get ready to step out and claim what God wanted to give them. God said in Joshua 1:2, "Get ready to cross the Jordan River into the land I am about to give [you]." He was leading them out of their comfort zone—but then He added His promise to be with them wherever they went.

Are *you* ready to move out of your comfort zone?

Are you ready to share the gospel with a neighbor?

Are you ready to teach a Sunday school class or lead a Bible study?

Are you ready to live out your faith where you work?

Open your life to God's will. Claim all that God wants to give you. Don't be afraid. Step out of your comfort zone. He will be with you!

Uninterrupted Praise

I will proclaim the name of the LORD. Oh, praise
the greatness of our God! He is the Rock, his
works are perfect, and all his ways are just.
Deuteronomy 32:3–4

The most powerful antidote for depression is praise—because it changes your perspective.

I wonder what the impact on the world would be if we began to practice uninterrupted praise of Christ?

Praise that's uninterrupted by our feelings, our fears, doubts, even our pain.

Praise that comes, not just in the choruses we sing, but also in the way we live our lives.

Praise in a world that's getting more hostile to the name of Jesus.

When you and I, as God's people, fill our lives with genuine, heartfelt praise, His glory comes down: the same glory that led the children of Israel through the wilderness, the same glory reflected on Moses' face, the same glory Ezekiel saw in the storm. God's glory comes down!

Open your heart to the power of praise. Start praising God now, and don't ever stop!

THE LIGHT OF JOY

I will sing to the LORD, for he has been good to me.
Psalm 13:6

Praise is often the key that turns defeat into victory ... even when your life seems to be sinking into darkness and despair and the enemy seems to have the upper hand.

As life gets more complicated and problems and pressures grow, don't forget the key!

Jehoshaphat, king of Judah, used the key when he "appointed men to sing to the LORD and to praise him for the splendor of his holiness as they went out at the head of the army, saying, 'Give thanks to the LORD, for his love endures forever.' As they began to sing and praise, the LORD set ambushes against the [enemy] ... and they were defeated" (2 Chronicles 20:21–22).

Paul and Silas, sitting in a Philippian jail, used the key. And as they sang praises, the prison doors were opened, the jailer was converted, and they were set free (Acts 16:25–36).

When you seem to be facing defeat ... when you feel imprisoned by ill health or by your circumstances ... when friends betray you and foes attack you ... it's time to use the key. It's time to start praising God!

FLOWING FREELY

Wash away all my iniquity and cleanse me from my sin.
Psalm 51:2

My mother ran a pipe into the mountainside where a spring flows near my parents' home. She put a wooden bucket under the pipe and a tin cup beside the pipe. When I hiked up the mountain, I'd stop for a drink. Sometimes the bucket would be half filled with stagnant water because something was blocking the pipe, stopping the water. Then Mother would run a stick through the pipe to dislodge whatever was stuck. And the water flowed freely once more!

Our lives are like the bucket. The Holy Spirit flows into our lives, and the only thing that restricts His filling us is our sin. The blockage has to be removed by confessing that sin so we're cleansed, and the water can flow again and fruit can be borne.

The Bible commands us to "be filled with the Spirit" (Ephesians 5:18). Let the water of the Holy Spirit flow into you and through you and into the lives of others. Confess and remove whatever is hindering the free flow of the Spirit in your life. Ask Him to fill you until you overflow!

THE HOLY SPIRIT'S MINISTRY

"I tell you the truth: It is for your good that I am
going away. Unless I go away, the Counselor will not
come to you; but if I go, I will send him to you."
John 16:7

Jesus' promise recorded in John 16:7 contains a name for the Holy
Spirit—Comforter—that reveals the uniqueness of His nearness to us.
It's equally translated from the Greek into six other names, each describing
a different aspect of the Holy Spirit's ministry in our lives:

Comforter: One who relieves another of mental distress.

Counselor: One who gives advice.

Helper: One who gives relief and support.

Advocate: One who pleads the cause of another.

Strengthener: One who causes you to become stronger, to endure and
resist attacks.

Standby: One who can always be relied on.

Isn't it reassuring to know you have Someone in your life with all these
attributes? That Someone is the Holy Spirit, who is Jesus in you!

EVERYTHING WE NEED FOR LIFE

His divine power has given us everything we need
for life and godliness through our knowledge of him
who called us by his own glory and goodness.

2 Peter 1:3

Never underestimate the power of God in your life. He is much bigger than you think and much greater than you think. Nothing is beyond His ability, whether it's a job-related problem, a marriage to reconcile, a memory to heal, a guilty conscience to cleanse, a sin to forgive, a budget to stretch, another mouth to feed, or anything else that may be troubling you.

When you have Jesus, you have everything you need. You have God's power to "fix" the broken things in your life. He is more than able to work out the difficulties in your marriage, your job, your finances, your memories, the loss of your house—everything! Ephesians 3:20 assures us that He "is able to do immeasurably more than all we ask or imagine."

Trust Him. He is greater than you think. He is able!

WATCH OUT!

*At once the Spirit sent him out into the desert, and he
was in the desert forty days, being tempted by Satan. He
was with the wild animals, and angels attended him.*
Mark 1:12–13

What incredible blessing has God given you?
In your ministry?

Your family?

Your career?

Your reputation?

In your personal walk with Him?

Watch out! Very often following tremendous blessing, the enemy makes
his attack. In his gospel, Mark tells us that following God's public praise of
His Son, Jesus went into the desert and was tempted by Satan for forty days.
Satan times his attacks to strike when we're off guard—when we're relaxing
in a victory achieved or an honor received or a blessing enjoyed.

To overcome the enemy triumphantly, you must not go one step out of
your way to confront him or avoid him. But you must be alert! Arm yourself
in Christ. Depend on God in prayer. Take up the sword of God's Word, and
the enemy will be defeated!

THE TWILIGHT ZONE

> "I am the light of the world. Whoever follows me will
> never walk in darkness, but will have the light of life."
> *John 8:12*

It's amazing how easily we adjust to darkness. When you go into a dark theater, you grope around until your eyes adjust. And then the darkness becomes quite comfortable. But go back outside, and your eyes water and you're reaching for your sunglasses. The light actually hurts your eyes.

Our world lives in spiritual darkness, separated from God. Jesus said He is the Light of the world. But too often today, people become comfortable in their own personal twilight zone, where the goal becomes reducing the Light, or even extinguishing it altogether so they can stay comfortable. We see this happening in our schools, our governments, our social gatherings.

But the Light is stronger than darkness. In a world of comfortable darkness, stay out of the twilight. Walk in the Light. Then be a light to guide others out of the darkness.

KNOWING GOD

"Now this is eternal life: that they may know you, the
only true God, and Jesus Christ, whom you have sent."
John 17:3

You and I were created to walk and talk with God, to love and obey God, to listen to and learn from God, to glorify and enjoy God ... *forever*!

Knowing God in a personal and permanent relationship is the ultimate human experience. It is the meaning of human life, the reason for our existence.

In the very beginning of creation, the relationship between God and Adam and Eve was the completion of what God had created. Your close, personal relationship with God is the completion of all the changes He is making in your life right now.

Walk with Him. Love Him. Trust Him with all your heart. Get to know Him.

Discover the real meaning to life!

STICKING OUT ALL OVER

We pray this so that the name of our Lord Jesus may
be glorified in you, and you in him, according to the
grace of our God and the Lord Jesus Christ.
2 Thessalonians 1:12

After the sermon, when the pastor was giving an invitation for people to invite Jesus to come into their hearts, a young boy stopped him. Perplexed, the boy said, "But Jesus is a man in a man's body."

"That's right," the pastor said patiently.

The boy persisted. "But I'm just a little boy."

The pastor nodded. "That's right."

Totally confused, the boy said, "If Jesus is a man, and He comes into my heart, He'll be sticking out all over!"

Grinning, the pastor said, "That's right!"

When Jesus Christ fills your life, others will see Him sticking out all over!

A Christian's ultimate aim in life is to bring glory to God. Yield your life completely to Jesus. Ask Him to fill you. And then give Him the glorious freedom to stick out all over!

TEMPTATION INTENSIFIES

"Watch and pray so that you will not fall into temptation.
The spirit is willing, but the body is weak."
Matthew 26:41

Knowing I love birthday cake, my friend dropped off two pieces from her own gooey birthday cake. But I was on a diet and didn't eat them—not immediately anyway! Then, after resisting the cake for a full day, I unwrapped the foil and ate both pieces at one sitting.

It actually made me feel sick! And it wasn't nearly as good as I had thought it would be.

The truth is, temptation intensifies as we tolerate it. The longer I looked at that cake, the more I wanted it. After resisting temptation all day, I almost felt I deserved to be rewarded by eating it! In Genesis 3:6, we're told that Eve saw the fruit, thought about it, touched it, and then "she took some and ate it."

What sin is tempting you? What temptation are you toying with? Thinking about? Looking at? Touching? One more glass of wine? A harmless flirtation? Watch out. Avoid living with the regret of having yielded to temptation. This is the time to pray!

SOMETHING MORE

How great is your goodness, which you have
stored up for those who fear you.
Psalm 31:19

Sometimes God is like the father of two little boys who tried to teach his sons a lesson. Off they went to the local discount store, where he said they could get whatever they wanted. First they wanted jellybeans.

"Are you sure?" Dad asked.

Rethinking their choice, the boys ran to the sporting section. Picking up a football, they said, "Daddy, this is it!"

He suggested they keep looking. They came to the bikes, and their eyes lit up. "Daddy, this is it. This is what we really want!"

Dad smiled. He'd intended to get them the bikes all along.

Could it be God hasn't given you what you've asked for because you've asked for jellybeans when He has a bicycle in mind? Maybe you're grieving now, but when you see what He has for you, your tears will be replaced by laughter. That's what Jesus was telling His disciples when He said, "You will grieve, but your grief will turn to joy" (John 16:20).

What God wants to give you is always more than you impulsively grab for yourself. Thank Him for sometimes saying no . . . so that He can say yes to something more.

AUGUST

Men ask for a rainbow in the cloud; but I would
ask more from Thee. I would be, in my cloud,
myself a rainbow … a minister to others' joy.

Mrs. Charles E. Cowman, *Streams in the Desert* (October 30)

ALL TO JESUS

"Bring the whole tithe into the storehouse, that there
may be food in my house. Test me in this," says the
LORD Almighty, "and see if I will not throw open the
floodgates of heaven and pour out so much blessing
that you will not have room enough for it."

Malachi 3:10

When Jesus asked Philip to take care of the lunch needs of the five
thousand people gathered to hear Him, Philip was appalled. He said,
"Eight months' wages would not buy enough bread for each one to have
even a bite!" (John 6:7).

But then Andrew, Simon Peter's brother, spoke up: "Here is a boy with
five small barley loaves and two small fish, but how far will they go?" (John
6:8–9).

Without realizing it, Andrew had found the key to the storehouse of
God's *ample* supply. When he offered Jesus a few loaves and fish, he was
offering Jesus everything he had.

What is it you have to offer? A little bit of your time? A little bit of your
love? A little bit of your money? A little bit of faith? Don't concentrate on
what you don't have. Concentrate on what you do have.

Give it all to Jesus. He will make it enough.

YOUR MOST PRECIOUS POSSESSION

Mary took about a pint of pure nard, an expensive perfume;
she poured it on Jesus' feet and wiped his feet with her hair.
John 12:3

I'm not a person who uses expensive perfume, but its extravagance isn't lost on me. In John 12:3, Mary takes an alabaster jar containing a fortune in perfumed ointment and pours the contents on Jesus' head and feet.

In her act of loving devotion, Mary gave Jesus everything. Her future. Her security. Her reputation. Her pride. And John 12:3 goes on to say, "The house was filled with the fragrance of the perfume."

Mary's selfless act of worship blessed her home, and the story has inspired thousands of others since that day some two thousand years ago.

What's *your* alabaster jar, your most precious possession?

Your children?

Your marriage?

Your career?

Your plans for the future?

Your time?

Would you be willing to break that jar open and pour it at Jesus' feet?

Fill your home with the fragrance of your sacrificial love for Jesus. Why? Because Jesus is heaven's alabaster jar, broken and poured out for you!

HE GIVES GOOD GIFTS

And you also were included in Christ when you
heard the word of truth, the gospel of your
salvation. Having believed, you were marked in
him with a seal, the promised Holy Spirit.
Ephesians 1:13

If you're a mother, it isn't likely you'll forget the births of your children! My children are grown, but I'm still thinking about what gifts I can give them for their birthdays that will cause their eyes to light up.

Jesus used that very example to encourage His disciples. He said, "If you, then, ... know how to give good gifts to your children, how much more will your Father in heaven give the Holy Spirit to those who ask Him!" (Luke 11:13). God wants to give you this incomparable gift—but you have to ask.

And John 14:16 adds that when God gives you this Gift, He will be with you forever. One reason you can be assured of never losing your salvation is that the seal of God in the person of the Holy Spirit cannot be broken.

Praise God! The Holy Spirit is the best Gift! He will never leave or forsake you!

A Desire to Be Holy

If the part of the dough offered as firstfruits is holy, then the
whole batch is holy; if the root is holy, so are the branches.
Romans 11:16

Sometimes we overlook the obvious—that the Holy Spirit is holy. And one of the first things the Holy Spirit does is to give us a desire to be holy too.

One Christmas I was looking for a pair of pj's for my daughter. I found the perfect top from one set and the perfect bottom from another. So I very quickly switched the tops and bottoms of the two sets. I left the store feeling quite pleased. But by the time I got home, I was miserable.

The next morning I went back to the store and confessed what I'd done. The clerk was astonished and not happy. But it was an incredible lesson that gave me an acute awareness of the Holy Spirit in my life. He'd refused to tolerate my deceitful behavior. And I am most grateful!

God is holy! And He works in our lives to make us holy too!

ACTIVATE THE POWER!

"You will receive power when the Holy Spirit comes on you; and you will be my witnesses in Jerusalem, and in all Judea and Samaria, and to the ends of the earth."

Acts 1:8

A man told the store clerk a huge oak tree had fallen on his roof. He needed the best chain saw the store carried, he said. The clerk immediately recommended a chain saw that he promised would "cut through that tree like soft butter." So the man bought it.

But several days later, the man was back. He said, "I've tried for two days, and the saw doesn't work."

The clerk reached down and pulled a little black cord—and the chain saw came alive! The man exclaimed in amazement, "What's that noise?"

He had been trying to use the saw without activating the power!

It's like someone trying to live the Christian life without ever activating the power. That power is not a *what* but a *who*. And that who is the Holy Spirit!

Do you think the Christian life doesn't work? Then isn't it time you activated the power? Yield your life to the Holy Spirit!

ALL IS WELL

> In the year that King Uzziah died, I saw the
> Lord seated on a throne, high and exalted.
> *Isaiah 6:1*

Are you living out a picture you never dreamed would be yours? A picture of poor health? A lost job? A spouse with cancer?

Recently I was reminded of 1 Samuel 2:7: "The LORD sends poverty and wealth; he humbles and he exalts." Yet in every season of life, amid poverty or wealth, sickness or health, the Lord is there.

When stress mounts in your life, the Lord is there. When pain wracks your body, the Lord is there. When grief breaks your heart, the Lord is there. When disappointment shatters your spirit, the Lord is there.

When you are going through hard times, experiencing more pressure than you think you can bear, remember that your hope does not rest in your ability to cling to Him but in His power to hold on to *you*!

He is your shield. Your hiding place. He is with you. He is seated on the throne. *He's* in control! All is well.

SPIRITUAL REST

The LORD is my shepherd, I shall not be in
want. He makes me lie down in green pastures,
he leads me beside quiet waters.
Psalm 23:1–2

Have you ever complained to your doctor, "Something's wrong. What's the matter with me?" Perhaps after an examination the doctor concludes, "You just need a rest."

All of us need to take a break from time to time, but my real concern is that I not become weary in my spirit. I need to make not just physical rest, but *spiritual* rest, a priority! Henry Drummond, an old-time revivalist, explained that spiritual rest "is not a hallowed feeling that comes over us in church. It's the repose of a heart set deep in God."

Psalm 116:7 says, "Be at rest once more, O my soul, for the LORD has been good to you." Do you need that kind of rest? Rest from burnout? Rest from trying to please God by your own efforts? Rest from worry, fear, or anger?

Be at rest. Lay your burdens at the feet of Jesus. Stop striving, and start trusting the Lord, who has been good to you.

TAKE A RISK

The Sovereign LORD is my strength; he makes my feet like
the feet of a deer, he enables me to go on the heights.
Habakkuk 3:19

In 2 Timothy 1:7, God reminds us He has not given us a spirit of timidity but a spirit of power. Living a life of faith requires taking risks—at least from our perspective—because we can't physically see what's ahead, or hear what God is saying, or know what He's thinking.

Frankly, the older I get, the less I want to take risks. I find myself holding the railing as I walk down stairs. I look both ways before driving through an intersection. In fact, I look *twice*!

Being cautious in everyday life can help you avoid accidents. But a cautious attitude in your spiritual life can paralyze your faith. It can cause you to procrastinate until obedience becomes a burden. Or worse, it can lead to disobedience.

So … take a *risk* of faith. Step out of your comfort zone. When God calls, it will be the surest, safest step you can take!

TRUST HIM WHEN YOU
DON'T UNDERSTAND

*These were all commended for their faith, yet none of them received
what had been promised. God had planned something better for
us so that only together with us would they be made perfect.*
Hebrews 11:39–40

There's no question, sometimes God's ways seem difficult to understand. Maybe you've suffered the death of a child, the betrayal of a spouse, or an illness that's threatened your life. Do you need a reminder to trust God even when you don't understand? Even when nothing seems to make sense?

In Romans 8:28, Paul wrote, "We know that in all things God works for the good of those who love him, who have been called according to his purpose." Paul was reminding the children of God that they can be confident that *all things* work together for good, that brokenness leads to blessing, that death leads to life, and that suffering leads to glory.

God gives meaning to your meaninglessness, hope to your hopelessness, reason to senselessness, and deliverance from bitterness.

So ... trust Him, even when you don't understand. He knows what He's doing!

GOD IS THERE

This is what the LORD says ... "Fear not, for I have redeemed
you; I have summoned you by name; you are mine.
When you pass through the waters, I will be with you."
Isaiah 43:1–2

Do you need answers, but God seems to be silent? In John 11, Mary and Martha sent word to Jesus, hoping He would heal their brother, Lazarus. They knew Jesus loved him. But Jesus didn't answer them! In fact, when they sent for Him, He stayed where He was two more days—and Lazarus died.

When Jesus finally came to Bethany, Martha said, "Lord, ... if you had been here, my brother would not have died" (John 11:21). Yet Jesus *did* come into Martha's place of grief, but He came in His own way, in His own time, and for His own purpose.

Today He promises you and me that He will do the same. He will be there with you in the midst of suffering. In Psalm 23:4, King David bore witness to God's presence: "Even though I walk through the valley of the shadow of death, I will fear no evil, for you are with me."

Jesus was with Mary and Martha in their grief, and ultimately He raised Lazarus from the dead. His delays in our lives develop our faith.

So exercise your faith! Trust in Him. His presence is there with you ... right now! How do you know? Because He says so.

ENJOY FORGIVENESS

Therefore, my brothers, I want you to know that through
Jesus the forgiveness of sins is proclaimed to you.
Acts 13:38

Did you know? There's nothing you've ever done that God cannot, or will not, forgive. It doesn't matter how big the sin or how small. It doesn't matter how long ago it was committed, or how recently. It doesn't matter whether it was spontaneous or malicious. It *doesn't* matter!

God *will* forgive you if you come to Him at the cross of His Son, Jesus Christ.

First John 1:9 promises, "If we confess our sins, he is faithful and just, and will forgive us our sins and purify us from all unrighteousness."

What do you think is beyond the forgiveness of God? Abortion? Adultery? Hate? Hypocrisy? Doubt? Worry? There's *nothing* you've ever done that God cannot or will not forgive when you humbly ask Him.

So confess your sin to Him personally, specifically, and honestly. Then ... enjoy living in your forgiveness!

GOD IS GOOD

Surely God is good.
Psalm 73:1

God is *good*! But is someone trying to convince you He isn't? That He doesn't have your best interest in mind? That He's somehow holding out on you?

We're never more vulnerable to this temptation than when our hearts are broken, when we cry out to God only to have Him remain silent. Or when we cry out to Him and experience a bad situation getting worse.

God is not deaf or indifferent, mean or unable to act. God cannot be less than Himself. And God *is* good. And active. And faithful. And He cares.

God loves you! Second Peter 1:3 says, "His divine power has given us everything we need for life and godliness through our knowledge of him who called us by his own glory and goodness."

When you can't understand what He is doing or why He is *not* doing something, put your faith in who the Bible reveals Him to be. Answer His call to know Him as He is. And you will experience peace. Because God is good!

LIVING HOPE

Record my lament; list my tears on your
scroll—are they not in your record?
Psalm 56:8

D o you feel like you're standing on the edge of a cliff? Are you dreading
tomorrow? Do you feel caught up in events beyond your control?

Regardless of what those events may be, no matter your mental or emotional or spiritual state, God's vision of the future can fill you with hope—*now*! Even if you're facing death. If you're lonely, isolated, cut off from family and friends.

You may be facing the greatest unknown of your life and you're feeling scared. If you're feeling hopeless for *any* reason—be encouraged! Jeremiah 29:11 says, "'For I know the plans I have for you,' declares the LORD, 'plans to prosper you and not to harm you, plans to give you hope and a future.'"

Praise God! Look forward with hope. Jesus rose from the dead and opened heaven for you, so you have the blessed assurance of one day going home!

YOUR DREAMS WILL COME TRUE

And I heard a loud voice from the throne saying,
"Now the dwelling of God is with men, and he will
live with them. They will be his people, and God
himself will be with them and be their God."

Revelation 21:3

What's your dream of heaven? As a young girl, my vision of heaven was framed by my mother's assurance that whatever was necessary for my eternal happiness would be there. In my child's mind, that meant ocean waves, mountain peaks, a favorite pet that had died, Sunday-night Bible games with my family, sleepovers at my grandparents' house, Chinese food, and a smaller nose!

Over the years, my requirements for eternal happiness have changed, but my dreams are still big. I love John's description of heaven in Revelation 21:1–2: "Then I saw a new heaven and a new earth... I saw the Holy City ... coming down out of heaven from God, prepared as a bride beautifully dressed for her husband."

Just as a bride lovingly prepares every detail of herself for her special bridegroom, God is preparing His heavenly home for you and me. One day our dreams will come true!

THE HOME OF YOUR DREAMS

*No longer will there be any curse. The throne of God and of
the Lamb will be in the city, and his servants will serve him.
They will see his face, and his name will be on their foreheads.*
Revelation 22:3–4

How are you suffering today? Physically? Emotionally? Mentally? Financially? I have good news for you! Someday there will be no more death or mourning or crying or pain. Revelation 21:4 says, "The old order of things has passed away."

Heaven will not only look fresh and new; it will *feel* fresh and new because God is there. One day, God Himself will take your face in His hands and gently wipe away your tears. He will assure you there will be no more suffering or things that cause it. No more cancer, no hospitals, no feared diagnosis. No terrorists, no wars, no guns or bombs. No more meanness or cruelty or betrayal. No more divorce or death.

You can look forward with hope because one day there will be no more suffering, no more separation, no more scars on your body or on your heart. None! You'll be in your Father's house. And it will be the home of your dreams! So ... keep looking up!

WHAT ARE YOUR PRIORITIES?

"And everyone who has left houses or brothers or sisters or
father or mother or children or fields for my sake will receive
a hundred times as much and will inherit eternal life."
Matthew 19:29

What are your priorities? What do you spend your time and money on? So many things get our top priority here that will have no value in eternity. It's sobering to think how much time, effort, sacrifice, compromise, and attention we give to acquiring and increasing our supply of things that will be totally insignificant in heaven.

So again, what *are* your priorities? And as you live them out, do they have *eternal* value? Jesus commanded His disciples in Matthew 6:19–20, "Do not store up for yourselves treasures on earth, where moth and rust destroy, and where thieves break in and steal. But store up for yourselves treasures in heaven." The Bible also says where your heart is, *there* will be your treasure (Matthew 6:21).

Do you need a change of heart? Instead of working to increase your portfolio here, what will you do now to increase your assets in heaven?

TEACH YOUR CHILDREN

Jesus called the children to him and said, "Let the
little children come to me, and do not hinder them,
for the kingdom of God belongs to such as these."
Luke 18:16

The Bible says we're to teach our children God's Word. Deuteronomy 11:19 says, "Teach them ... when you sit at home and when you walk along the road, when you lie down and when you get up."

When my children were young, it was a challenge morning after morning to get their attention for daily Bible reading and prayer. It just wasn't at the top of their to-do list! I took them to Sunday school and church. I read Bible stories to them and tried to explain the simplest truths of God's Word. My effort was rewarded when each of my children later responded by claiming Jesus personally as their Savior.

Praise God! The investment in your children's spiritual good is an investment for eternity. So even if Bible reading and prayer are not on *their* list of priorities, put them at the top of *yours*!

THE OBJECT OF YOUR FAITH

Yet I am not ashamed, because I know whom I have
believed, and am convinced that he is able to guard
what I have entrusted to him for that day.

2 Timothy 1:12

Do you know what you believe? And why you believe it? Do you know
who you believe? Can you discern truth based on God's Word? If your
faith is based on what others say or think or do—if your faith is based on
secondhand information—it will be weak. It will not stand up to storms,
attacks, and heavy pressure.

The real problem may be your understanding, even ignorance, of who
God truly is and what He's actually said—how He works. In Matthew 17:20,
Jesus said, "I tell you the truth, if you have faith as small as a mustard seed,
you can say to this mountain, 'Move from here to there' and it will move.
Nothing will be impossible for you."

In other words, it's not the amount of your faith that makes the difference. It's the object of your faith. Place all of your faith in God and God
alone. Then ... watch the mountains move!

A CONTRITE HEART

The sacrifices of God are a broken spirit; a broken
and contrite heart, O God, you will not despise.
Psalm 51:17

There is pleasure in sin … for a season. Then the "aftertaste" leaves bitterness and guilt. David was called a man after God's own heart, but he was also a sinner. When he saw his neighbor's wife, Bathsheba, he sent for her. He slept with her, and Bathsheba became pregnant. To cover up the adultery, David ordered her husband to the front lines of battle, and he was killed.

Things went well for David—at first. He had pleasure in sin. But then his guilt ate at him until he poured out his confession to his heavenly Father. Psalm 51:3–4 records David's cry to God: "For I know my transgressions, and my sin is always before me. Against you, you only, have I sinned." David's sin was not just against Bathsheba or her husband or even himself. It was against God.

What guilt is eating at you? What unconfessed sin is keeping you from the fullness of God's blessing? Cry out to God now. If He would forgive David, and He did, He will forgive you!

A HARVEST OF RIGHTEOUSNESS

Now he who supplies seed to the sower and bread for
food will also supply and increase your store of seed
and will enlarge the harvest of your righteousness.
2 Corinthians 9:10

When it comes to misery and weariness, we have a choice in how we handle it. Paul told the Galatian church in Galatians 6:9: "Let us not become weary in doing good, for at the proper time we will reap a harvest if we do not give up."

One way to overcome misery and weariness is to keep your focus on the big picture. As hard as your life is, as challenging as your problems and pressures may be, don't give up. Don't quit. Your effort to live for Jesus and to serve Jesus are like long-term investments. You may not reap the benefits now, but you will in time.

What harvest of blessing and fruit and glory will you reap later because you choose now not to give in to your weariness? Keep looking up, as you keep on keeping on ...

YOUR INHERITANCE

Praise be to the God and Father of our Lord Jesus Christ! In
his great mercy he has given us new birth into a living hope
through the resurrection of Jesus Christ from the dead.

1 Peter 1:3

You have an inheritance! An inheritance the Bible confirms will "never perish, spoil or fade" (1 Peter 1:4). It's being kept in heaven for you, and although that inheritance is safely stored in heaven, there is a condition you have to meet before you can claim it. Revelation 21:7 says, "He who overcomes will inherit all this, and I will be his God and he will be my son."

So what do you have to overcome? You have to overcome your pride—a pride that refuses to acknowledge you're a sinner who needs a Savior. A pride that insists if you do more good works than bad works, God will let you into His heavenly home.

And you have to overcome your unbelief that rejects Jesus as the only way to God.

Is it worth clinging to your pride and unbelief and forfeiting your inheritance? Think about it. In the long run, from eternity's perspective, which will be worth more?

DON'T PRETEND

And we, who with unveiled faces all reflect the Lord's glory,
are being transformed into his likeness with ever-increasing
glory, which comes from the Lord, who is the Spirit.
2 Corinthians 3:18

You and I will never be perfect. And what's even more significant—we don't have to be! Psalm 53:3 says, "There is no one who does good, not even one."

Inadequacy and inferiority can be great blessings because they make us dependent on God. And God uses those who depend on Him.

When I honestly confess my inadequacy, it's as though I hear God whispering, "Anne, it's okay. I know you are inadequate. But I am sufficient. Lean on Me!" When I stand at the foot of the cross, when I take a good look at who Jesus is, how can I feel inferior? God loves me so much He gave His own Son's life for me.

And He loves you just as much. You don't have to be someone you're not. You can be yourself—shortcomings and failures included.

Don't pretend to be better than you are. Surrender your life to Him and ask Him to make you who He wants you to be! Then give Him the glory!

GOD'S WORD RENEWS US

*I am laid low in the dust; preserve my
life according to your word.*
Psalm 119:25

Y ou may be going through the most difficult time in your life, but let me
encourage you that God's Word will sustain you—as it has sustained
me. The pressures of pain and suffering, my son's cancer, the loss of my
mother and father, my husband's illness and death—through it all, God
sustains me. And He will sustain you too. Isaiah 50:4 says, "He wakens me
morning by morning, wakens my ear to listen like one being taught."

Some days I'm only capable of reading a verse at a time. Yet the supernatural, life-giving power of God's Word penetrates my suffering and
emotional upheaval, giving me strength to go on—one day at a time.

Colossians 3:16 says, "Let the word of Christ dwell in you richly."

Claim His strength. His peace. Hang on to His hope. His power. All
that He is, is available to you and me through His Word. There is renewal
of life in God's Word. So ... read your Bible.

THE ULTIMATE PRIVILEGE

For through him we both have access
to the Father by one Spirit.
Ephesians 2:18

Have you ever watched a royal wedding? It is obviously an event only the *privileged* are invited to attend. But when you come to God, believing in Jesus' name—you enter a world of *ultimate* privilege. Doors open, angels attend, doubts disappear, and fears fade. And the God of the universe bends down to hear what you have to say.

Romans 8:34 says, "Christ Jesus, who died … who was raised to life—is at the right hand of God, and is also interceding for us." You don't have to have a priest; you don't have to go to a temple or make a donation. And you don't have to live on the right side of town or dress fashionably or speak correctly.

In Christ, you *are* a person of privilege! A child of God. You have immediate access, 24/7, to His presence. And you will be welcomed one day into your heavenly home. Enjoy your privileges!

LOSE YOUR LIFE

I will praise you as long as I live, and in your name I will lift
up my hands. My soul will be satisfied as with the richest
of foods; with singing lips my mouth will praise you.
Psalm 63:4–5

A re you leaving Jesus out of your plans? Are you excluding Him from your activities? Your business? Your decisions? If so, I wonder if you are a Christian who's saved but not satisfied? Could it be that, even though you're assured that your sins are forgiven and you're going to heaven, you're pretty much living for yourself?

In the long run, will you be disappointed?

Jesus said, "For whoever wants to save his life will lose it, but whoever loses his life for me will find it" (Matthew 16:25). There's a depth of satisfaction reserved for those who know Jesus as their Savior and who live their lives not for themselves, but for Him.

Will you lose out later because you're clinging to what you want today? Instead, let go of what you want and claim all He wants to give you. You will find the deep, lasting satisfaction that comes from living a life that's totally surrendered to Him. But you must lose your life—to gain it.

SEEING GOD

"I and the Father are one."
John 10:30

If you want to know what's on the mind of God, look at Jesus.
If you want to know the will of God, look at Jesus.

If you want to know what's in the heart of God, look at Jesus!

Jesus makes God visible. John 1:1–2 says Jesus was with God in the beginning, and that Jesus is God! Jesus was not more and not less than God. He is equally supreme, sharing the glory of heaven's throne, because Jesus and God are One.

What a wondrous mystery! Throughout the ages people have engaged in an intellectual wrestling match with this truth. But those who do so miss the blessing that comes from simply worshiping an infinite God who is beyond our understanding.

If you want to know the heart of God, look at Jesus. To see Jesus is to see God!

GOD CAN FILL YOU

For by him all things were created: things in
heaven and on earth, visible and invisible, whether
thrones or powers or rulers or authorities; all
things were created by him and for him.

Colossians 1:16

Is your heart broken? Does your life need mending? Jesus knows what's
wrong in your life and how to fix it.

In John 1:3, Jesus is described as One through whom "all things were
made; without him, nothing was made that has been made." Jesus, the creator of life, knows how to make life work. He created everything, and there's
nothing beyond His power to fix or mend, heal or restore.

God is the One who delivered His brokenhearted children from bondage in Egypt. Psalm 28:6 says, "Praise be to the LORD, for he has heard my
cry for mercy." Could it be God has not "fixed" you because you haven't
cried out to Him?

Let Him take charge of your life. Give Him the authority to put it right.
Give Him your broken heart. Cry out to the One who made you. Cry out
to Jesus!

LIVE IN THE LIGHT

The true light that gives light to every
man was coming into the world.
John 1:9

Jesus said, "I am the light of the world" (John 8:12). His life is literally our light! John 1:5 tells us that this light "shines in the darkness."

Darkness symbolizes everything that is *not* light: Untruth. Evil. Sin. Wrongdoing. Injustice. Ignorance. And unbelief. Have you adjusted your spiritual eyes to the dark? Are you content to see just well enough to get along in life?

Some people within the church seem to be sleepwalking when they should be on high alert. Their eyes seem to be blinded, ears deafened, minds numbed, and hearts hardened to the light.

We're teetering on the edge of a giant abyss where time stops and eternity begins. Yet we seem to have succumbed to the darkness, or at least to the murky twilight of living as though this life is all there is or ever will be. It's time to wake up! It's time to *see* the Light! Jesus is coming!

LET YOUR LIGHT SHINE

"In the same way, let your light shine before men, that they may see your good deeds and praise your Father in heaven."
Matthew 5:16

Darkness cannot overcome light! Light is stronger. But it *can* be hidden! The Bible says, "You are the light of the world. A city on a hill cannot be hidden. Neither do people light a lamp and put it under a bowl. Instead they put it on its stand, and it gives light to everyone in the house" (Matthew 5:14–15).

What is the bowl under which you are hiding the light? Is it a bowl of political correctness? The opinions of others? Are you so intimidated by the darkness that you're hiding the light of Jesus under a bowl of fear? Fear of being offensive? Or of being unpopular? Or of being criticized or made fun of? Don't hide the truth of the gospel! Throw away the bowl! Let His light shine!

GOD HEARS YOU

This is the confidence we have in approaching God: that
if we ask anything according to his will, he hears us.
1 John 5:14

The truth is, bad things happen to those Jesus loves. But you and I need to learn to interpret our circumstances by God's love—not interpret His love by our circumstances!

With all their wealth and influence, Mary, Martha, and their brother, Lazarus, were helpless in the face of Lazarus' serious illness. The sisters became so alarmed that they "sent word to Jesus, 'Lord, the one you love is sick'" (John 11:3). Jesus got their message, yet He stayed where He was two more days. In the face of His friends' urgent plea, He was silent and still.

Has your desperate prayer remained unanswered? Have you prayed, yet you seem to get no response or movement? Jesus' delay is never due to indifference or preoccupation, or an inability to act. His purpose is to develop your faith in Him and Him alone—until you display His glory. So stop doubting Him. He has heard your prayer, and He knows exactly how and when to answer it. He is always on time.

AMAZING GRACE

Grace and peace to you from God our
Father and the Lord Jesus Christ.
1 Corinthians 1:3

The Christian life isn't motivated by a list of dos and don'ts but by the gracious outpouring of God's grace and blessing. We don't deserve His grace. We can't earn it. We can't bargain for it. We can't buy it. We can only open our hearts and hands to receive it. It's the miracle of grace: **G**reat **R**iches **A**t **C**hrist's **E**xpense. For a lifetime. Forever!

John 1:17 says, "The law was given through Moses; grace and truth came through Jesus Christ." Jesus perfectly fulfills the law. Our lives don't. That's the truth. His life meets God's standard of perfection. But when we receive Jesus by faith, His righteousness is credited to us. That's grace! Grace that is greater than all our sin and guilt and shortcomings and mistakes and failures.

We are saved by grace. We stand in grace ... one blessing after another that we don't deserve! And that's amazing!

September

Great souls have great sorrows.... The capacity for knowing God enlarges as we are brought by Him into circumstances which oblige us to exercise faith.

Mrs. Charles E. Cowman, *Streams in the Desert* (November 3)

STAND UP AND SPEAK OUT

Then they called them in again and commanded them not
to speak or teach at all in the name of Jesus. But Peter and
John replied, "Judge for yourselves whether it is right in
God's sight to obey you rather than God. For we cannot
help speaking about what we have seen and heard."
Acts 4:18–20

Jesus said, "No servant is greater than his master. If they persecuted me, they will persecute you also" (John 15:20). And remember, they didn't just *persecute* Jesus. They crucified Him.

It's said more than forty-five million men and women during the twentieth century were put to death for their faith in Jesus Christ. In more recent times, the estimate of those being persecuted for their faith is around 215 million. Imagine! What's more, imagine an average of 90,000 Christians dying for their faith *every year.* Almost 250 a day!

This morning while you were getting up and trying to decide what to wear, what to eat, somewhere in the world, a man or woman, or child, was paying the ultimate price for his or her relationship with Jesus. Why do we cringe when someone simply raises an eyebrow when we mention our faith? It's time you and I had the courage to stand up and speak out for Jesus. If He is filling our hearts, how can we help it?

INVITE JESUS TO YOUR WEDDING

As a bridegroom rejoices over his bride,
so will your God rejoice over you.
Isaiah 62:5

Today is my wedding anniversary. How well I remember the challenge of compiling the guest list, which makes the scene in the second chapter of John very personal, as a wedding is taking place. "Jesus' mother was there, and Jesus and his disciples had also been invited" (John 2:1–2). Evidently their names were on the guest list, and they had accepted the invitation.

What about including Jesus in your wedding plans? In your marriage? My husband and I had our wedding bands inscribed with a triangle that signifies there are three of us in this relationship: God at the apex, Danny and me at the lower corners. As we grew closer to God individually, we also drew closer to each other. That principle took us through some bumpy territory. It will do the same for you.

If you need a miracle in your marriage, invite Jesus into the relationship. He'll be there when you need Him most. Send the invitation—do it today!

FIRSTHAND INFORMATION

That which was from the beginning, which we have
heard, which we have seen with our eyes, which
we have looked at and our hands have touched—
this we proclaim concerning the Word of life.

1 John 1:1

Are you basing your knowledge of Jesus on hearsay evidence? Is it based on what you've heard a pastor say, or your parents or friends say . . . or maybe someone in the media or in a book?

Many are willing to say that Jesus was a good man, even a great man, or even a prophet from God. But they stop short of truly being convinced that He is virgin-born, the unique, only begotten Son of God—God Himself in a man's body. They stop short of saying He is God's Lamb, sacrificed for the sin of the world . . . that He is the risen Lord, the reigning King. Yet God said in Mark 9:7, "This is my Son, whom I love. Listen to him!"

Stop getting information about Jesus secondhand. Get it firsthand by reading God's Word. Get to know Him for yourself.

MADE ALIVE!

But because of his great love for us, God, who is rich in mercy, made us alive with Christ even when we were dead in transgressions—it is by grace you have been saved.
Ephesians 2:4–5

When we're "born again" (John 3:7) we become alive spiritually, even though we may not understand it or be able to articulate what has happened. John 3:8 says it's like wind. It "blows wherever it pleases. You hear its sound, but you cannot tell where it comes from or where it is going. So it is with everyone born of the Spirit."

But could it be that, instead of being born again, you are one of the walking dead? Alive physically, but dead spiritually? John 3:36 says, "Whoever believes in the Son has eternal life, but whoever rejects the Son will not see life."

Jesus said, "Unless you are born again, you cannot see the Kingdom of God" (John 3:3 NLT). Wake up! Confess to God that you are a sinner, that you are sorry and you're willing to repent. Claim His Son Jesus as your personal Savior, and invite Him into your life. Don't let pride or unbelief or religiosity keep you from an authentic, personal relationship with the living God. You *must* be born again.

WHERE IS LOVE FOUND?

I pray that out of his glorious riches he may strengthen
you with power through his Spirit in your inner being, so
that Christ may dwell in your hearts through faith. And I
pray that you, being rooted and established in love, may
have power, together with all the saints, to grasp how
wide and long and high and deep is the love of Christ.
Ephesians 3:16–18

We need to love and be loved, but we look for love in all the wrong places. We look for it from a parent, a child, a sibling, a spouse, a lover, a friend—even a pet! But our parents grow old, our children grow up and live their own lives, our siblings move on, our spouses are too busy, our lovers become bored, our friends are selfish, and our pets can't speak or counsel!

So where *is* love found? John 3:16 says, "For God so loved the world that he gave his one and only Son." He gave heaven's most precious treasure as the price of your redemption so that you might have eternal life.

Jesus is the ultimate Gift, sent to you from the heart of the Father. The gift tag reads, "I love you." Love is found in Jesus!

EXAMINE YOUR WORSHIP

"Yet a time is coming and has now come when the true
worshipers will worship the Father in spirit and truth,
for they are the kind of worshipers the Father seeks."
John 4:23

God wants us to worship Him in truth. But what does that mean? Since Jesus said *He* is the truth, it means there's no way to God, no way at all, without coming through Jesus. And God's Word is the truth. There's no way we can worship God acceptably if we're not reading our Bibles.

John 4:24 says, "His worshipers *must* worship in spirit and in truth" (italics are mine). God also wants us to worship Him in spirit, which means to worship Him honestly, without hypocrisy, standing open and transparent before Him.

What needs correcting in your worship? Is your worship attitude more about "have to" than "want to"? Is it more about your church's rituals than your personal relationship with God through Jesus? If you want to truly worship God, you must—it's not an option—you must start worshiping Him as He says ... in spirit and in truth.

DRY AND THIRSTY

"Whoever believes in me, as the Scripture has said,
streams of living water will flow from within him."
John 7:38

In the busyness of responsibility, the demands of family, even the excitement of opportunity, we can find ourselves running on empty.

Then, when we wake up and realize, "I'm so dry and thirsty," we look closely and see the reason may be traced to one thing: we're not drinking freely of the Water of Life—God's Word! Are you neglecting your Bible reading? Rushing through your prayer time? Not listening to the voice of the Lord because you're just too busy to be still? If so, it's time to carve out a daily appointment with God so you can confess your sins, read and meditate on His Word, pray, and just drink Him in.

Jesus told the Samaritan woman at the well, "If you knew the gift of God and who it is that asks you for a drink, you would have asked him and he would have given you living water" (John 4:10). So now that you know how to relieve your thirst and refresh your spiritual life ... ask for a drink.

How Do You See People?

When Jesus landed and saw a large crowd, he had
compassion on them and healed their sick.
Matthew 14:14

When Jesus looked out at the crowds interrupting His day off, He saw people who longed for God. People who had rowed three miles across the lake or walked seven miles to reach Him. People who'd made a real effort to spend their time with Him.

To Jesus, the gathered people were "like sheep without a shepherd" (Matthew 9:36). Jesus was tired, but the people before Him were more important than His own plans and need for rest. Jesus saw people as God saw them. How do *you* see people? Especially those who interrupt your "me time" or who cause you irritation or frustration on busy days?

Ask God to help you see people through His eyes. Look at people from His point of view, as sheep who need the Shepherd. Then be willing to give your time and energy to help them find Him. Move your focus off yourself and onto the needs of others ... for Jesus' sake!

A GLEAMING SHOWCASE

God chose the foolish things of the world to shame the
wise; God chose the weak things of the world to shame
the strong. He chose the lowly things of this world and the
despised things—and the things that are not—to nullify
the things that are, so that no one may boast before him.
1 Corinthians 1:27–29

The apostle Paul pleaded with the Lord to take away his "thorn in the flesh" three times. Instead, the Lord answered, "My grace is sufficient for you, for my power is made perfect in weakness" (2 Corinthians 12:9).

Weakness gives God opportunities to display His strength ... His glory. What kind of weakness has caused you to suffer? Weak health? Weak finances? Weak family relationships?

Could it be God has given you a platform from which you can be a witness of His strength, His power and grace to those who are watching? If you're suffering, don't be ashamed. Praise God that He has chosen you to be a demonstration of His strength! Our ultimate aim in life is not to be healthy, wealthy, or problem free. Our ultimate aim is to bring glory to God. So ... delight in your weakness!

SOARING BY FAITH

He mounted the cherubim and flew; he
soared on the wings of the wind.
2 Samuel 22:11

W hat storm has swept into your life? The storm of death? Divorce? A
job loss? Bankruptcy? A rebellious child? How have you reacted to
the storm?

Instead of complaining, spread your wings of faith and allow the storm
to take you higher. In the midst of the storms, it's possible to experience
God's peace and His quiet "everyday" miracles. His joy will balance your
pain. His power will lift your burden. His peace will calm your worries. And His all-sufficiency will be more than adequate to meet all your
responsibilities.

What I'm discovering is that growth that results in depth and strength
and consistency—and ultimately in Christlikeness—is only possible when
the winds of life are contrary to my personal comfort. Isaiah 40:31 says,
"Those who hope in the LORD will renew their strength. They will soar on
wings like eagles." So ... spread your wings and soar like an eagle in your
faith.

HIGH ALERT

Be self-controlled and alert. Your enemy the devil prowls
around like a roaring lion looking for someone to devour.
1 Peter 5:8

Ever since 9/11, our eyes have been opened to an enemy who uses terror as a weapon aimed at achieving our destruction. As Christians, we have an even deadlier enemy dedicated to our utter destruction, and yet we seem to be indifferent to the danger.

But God commands us to be on high alert, warning us of the attacks we face from the enemy of our souls. He also has given us instructions on how to not only defend and protect ourselves, but also how to seize the offensive.

Ephesians 6:10–11 says, "Be strong in the Lord and in his mighty power. Put on the full armor of God so that you can take your stand against the devil's schemes."

Be alert. Be assured. And praise Jesus that the ultimate victory, through Christ, has already been won!

AGREE WITH GOD

Take words with you and return to the LORD. Say to
him: "Forgive all our sins and receive us graciously,
that we may offer the fruit of our lips."
Hosea 14:2

Only God has the power to forgive sin. He promises in 1 John 1:9, "If we confess our sin, he is faithful and just and will forgive us our sins and purify us from all unrighteousness." *Confess* means to call sin by the same name that God does. To agree with Him that your sin is not *worry*—it's lack of faith. It's not *exaggeration*—it's lying. It's not *gossip*—it's slander. It's not *safe sex*—it's fornication or adultery.

When we switch the labels of sin to make it seem less serious, we're being dishonest with ourselves and with God. It doesn't matter if the sin is big or small. It doesn't matter if it was committed long ago or recently. It doesn't matter whether it was spontaneous or malicious. God will forgive you. But you must say the same thing about your sin that God says about it!

So come. Agree with Him. Confess honestly. Be forgiven today.

ARE YOU GUILTY?

If an enemy were insulting me, I could endure it; if a
foe were raising himself against me, I could hide from
him. But it is you, a man like myself, my companion, my
close friend, with whom I once enjoyed sweet fellowship
as we walked with the throng at the house of God.
Psalm 55:12–14

Are you guilty of the sin of betrayal? Not just betraying another person, but also your Lord?

You and I betray Jesus when we call ourselves Christians and yet give our hearts to money, or to selfish pursuits, or to anyone or anything other than fully to Him.

We betray Him when we spend more time on the Internet than in prayer. We betray Him when we spend more time reading the news than reading the Bible. We betray Him when we exercise our spiritual gift, not in a way that serves Christ and His body, but in a way that serves ourselves.

If you've betrayed Jesus, pray, "Jesus, I'm so sorry I've betrayed you. Please forgive me." First John 1:9 says, "If we confess our sins, he is faithful and just and will forgive us our sins and purify us from all unrighteousness." You are forgiven! Go . . . and sin no more.

THE LOVE OF GOD

"The Father himself loves you because you have loved
me and have believed that I came from God."
John 16:27

Who's giving you a rough time because you're trusting God, saying things like, "If God really loved you, He would heal you"? Or, "If God really loved you, He wouldn't have allowed you to lose your job"? Or, "If God really loved you, He would bring your spouse back"?

It's wicked for others to make you doubt God's love. The proof of His love is the cross. Romans 5:8 says, "God demonstrates His own love toward us, in that while we were still sinners, Christ died for us" (NKJV).

The cruelest of the taunts hurled at Jesus on the cross was surely the suggestion that included the words "*if* he is the Christ of God, the Chosen One" (Luke 23:35, italics mine). In other words, if God really loved Jesus, He wouldn't have allowed His Son to be in that situation.

But even in the blackness of the hate around the cross, the love of God broke through like the rays of the sun! If God *really* loved you? There's no *if* about it. God loves you.

God loves you!

LIFE'S PURPOSE

"For I know the plans I have for you," declares
the LORD, "plans to prosper you and not to harm
you, plans to give you hope and a future."
Jeremiah 29:11

This may be the best news you'll hear all day: God has a wonderful purpose for your life!

Jesus described that purpose when He said, "You did not choose me, but I chose you and appointed you to go and bear fruit—fruit that will last. Then the Father will give you whatever you ask in my name. This is my command: Love each other" (John 15:16–17).

God has chosen you to bear fruit. And that fruit is in your Holy Spirit–given character, which is love, joy, peace, patience, kindness, goodness, faithfulness, gentleness, and self-control (Galatians 5:22–23). It's simply the character of Jesus coming out through you. It's your service as you lead others to faith in Jesus Christ, as you help them grow into maturity so they'll also bear fruit.

Your life has eternal significance. Don't miss out on God's plans for your future.

WAIT FOR THE LORD

Wait for the LORD; be strong and take
heart and wait for the LORD.
Psalm 27:14

Waiting may be one of the ultimate tests of our faith. It certainly is one of the hardest spiritual disciplines to learn.

Isaiah wisely encouraged those who are waiting on God to consider others who have waited on Him. He pointed out in Isaiah 64:4, "Since ancient times no one has heard, no ear has perceived, no eye has seen any God besides you, who acts on behalf of those who wait for him."

Scripture says if we wait on God we will be blessed. If we grow impatient while waiting and take matters into our own hands, we'll be in trouble.

Are you waiting on God for something? Then take heart. Don't run ahead. Be strong enough to wait. Wait. And again I say, wait for the Lord.

HEAVENLY BREAD

Then Jesus declared, "I am the bread of life. He
who comes to me will never go hungry, and he
who believes in me will never be thirsty."

John 6:35

As Jesus spoke with the apostle Peter after the resurrection, He told Peter the same thing three times with slightly different words: "Feed my lambs" … "Take care of my sheep" … "Feed my sheep" (John 21:15–17). Sometimes we need repetition, don't we? It's good to be reminded of the importance of "feeding" the children—and adults—in our lives with God's Word.

Who are the lambs He wants you to feed? Could they be the children who keep flocking into your backyard to play with your children? Or the children who are in Sunday school classes at your church, or your children's friends who sleep over at your home? Ask God to give you creativity in getting His Word into their minds and hearts.

And who are the sheep He wants you to care for and feed? Maybe they are the older people in your church or your neighborhood. They can feed themselves if you provide a "green pasture"—a Bible class, home study, small group, or Sunday school.

Jesus said if you love Him, you will feed His "lambs" and feed His "sheep." Do you love Jesus? Then it's time to get busy…

Go All the Way

"In the same way, any of you who does not give
up everything he has cannot be my disciple."
Luke 14:33

What's your place of compromise on your journey with the Lord? Did you stop "halfway" because of the demands of your job? The birth of a baby? The opinions of others? Are you "halfway" to a vibrant relationship with God?

When God called Abraham to follow Him in a life of obedient faith, He commanded, "Leave your country, your people and your father's household... and I will bless you" (Genesis 12:1–2).

It's not an option. Be willing to leave everything—not *half* of everything, but *everything* if we want to truly know and follow Him. That means leaving what's familiar, abandoning any fence-sitting you're doing. And yes, even giving up the fear of living a life that will be very different from the lives of people around you.

Begin the adventure of stepping out of your comfort zone. Begin the adventure of truly experiencing God in a personal, authentic, vibrant relationship. Go all the way. Embrace a God-filled life!

SEEK HIS FACE

One thing I ask of the LORD, this is what I seek: that I may
dwell in the house of the LORD all the days of my life, to gaze
upon the beauty of the LORD and to seek him in his temple.

Psalm 27:4

When Jesus said to Peter, "Follow me!" Peter pointed to another apostle standing nearby and asked Jesus, "'Lord, what about him?' Jesus answered, '. . . What is that to you? *You* must follow me'" (John 21:19, 21–22, italics are mine).

Jesus also says bluntly to you and me that we are to get our eyes off that other person and keep our focus on Him. Have you been deeply disturbed and discouraged, even depressed, as you have looked at the lives of those who say they are disciples yet they live like unbelievers? You wonder, *Where is the purity? The integrity? The humility? The commitment to unity with other believers?*

My prayer is that if Jesus cannot be seen in *them*, I want Him to be seen in *me*. Don't live your life in comparison with others. Don't look at other people and institutions and organizations or even churches! Don't be deceived by other religions. Keep your focus on Jesus. Follow Him.

MAKE TIME

One of those days Jesus went out to a mountainside
to pray, and spent the night praying to God.
Luke 6:12

I don't have time to read my Bible." "I don't have time to pray." Sound familiar? I've said those same words myself. I stay busy, so I have to *make* time to read God's Word, to study it, to apply it and live by it ... and to pray.

Mark 6 tells us about a time when Jesus' disciples were on an emotional roller coaster, to say the least: bombarded with the brutal beheading of John the Baptist, thrilled by experiencing the power of God to change lives through their ministry, and exhausted and having no time to even eat because of the demands on their time. But Jesus understood. He said, "Come with me by yourselves" (v. 31).

You and I are given that same invitation! The catch? We have to *choose* to accept His invitation and make the time to be with Him.

Accept His invitation. Set your alarm. Carve out time in your daily schedule. Draw aside with Jesus!

DON'T QUIT

"Even now," declares the LORD, "return to me with all
your heart, with fasting and weeping and mourning."
Joel 2:12

When you fail—don't quit! This is one lesson we learn from Abraham. In all of history, few names are greater than that of Abraham—the father of the Jews, the father of the Arabs, and the father of faith for Christians. Yet we see that again and again Abraham's life was marked by failure, including lying and adultery.

But the reason we associate Abraham with faith and friendship with God is because when he failed, he didn't quit! He returned to the altar, got right with God, and kept moving forward.

Have you failed? Are you tempted to quit? Hebrews 10:35–36 says, "Do not throw away your confidence; it will be richly rewarded. You need to persevere so that when you have done the will of God, you will receive what he has promised."

Don't quit! Instead, return to the altar of the cross. Get right with God. Then keep going forward.

TEACHING BY EXAMPLE

I am not ashamed of the gospel, because it is the
power of God for the salvation of everyone who
believes: first for the Jew, then for the Gentile.

Romans 1:16

What are you teaching by your example? When you think about the lessons you're offering others, consider what the apostle Paul taught Timothy. He told him, "But as for you, continue in what you have learned and have become convinced of, because you know those from whom you learned it, and how from infancy you have known the holy Scriptures, which are able to make you wise for salvation through faith in Christ Jesus" (2 Timothy 3:14–15).

Encourage your children to be in God's Word. Make sure they see you studying it, reading it, praying it! And if you don't have children of your own, ask God whom you can challenge and encourage the way Paul did Timothy.

Give those you influence an example of someone who is not only a student of the Scriptures but a person who lives them out. Someone who is not ashamed of the gospel. Someone whose faith is contagious.

A HEART EXPOSED

O LORD, you have searched me and you know
me. You know when I sit and when I rise;
you perceive my thoughts from afar.
Psalm 139:1–2

Is there a wall around your heart? A wall of pride or doubt, shame or anger? Did you think if you opened your heart and let God see inside He would blame you for what He finds there? Or for what He doesn't find? That He would fault you for your lack of faith?

In Psalm 139:23–24, David prayed: "Search me, O God, and know my heart; test me, and know my anxious thoughts. See if there is any offensive way in me, and lead me in the way everlasting." You can't hide anything from God—not your thoughts, your feelings, or your desires. Why would you want to? You and I can be so foolish!

Open up your heart. Expose it to Him. It takes courage to let Him see exactly how you feel, what you think, what you want. But don't hide what's in your heart or pretend it's not there. Open it all up to Him. He will cleanse you ... and give you peace.

THE POTTER

I went down to the potter's house, and I saw him working
at the wheel. But the pot he was shaping from the
clay was marred in his hands; so the potter formed it
into another pot, shaping it as seemed best to him.
Jeremiah 18:3–4

I f you're a child of God and going through a difficult time, know that your suffering isn't wasted. God is molding you—and remolding you—in His image, and He knows exactly what He is doing. The apostle Paul reminds us that "our light and momentary troubles are achieving for us an eternal glory that far outweighs them all" (2 Corinthians 4:17).

The spiritual principle is that in some way God uses suffering to transform ordinary, dust-clay people like us into vessels that are strong in faith, vessels that are fit for His use, vessels that display His glory to the watching world.

Are you feeling pressure? Stress? Are you suffering hurt or heartache? Illness or injustice? Don't waste your sorrow! In these momentary troubles you *are* achieving an eternal glory. Praise God! He is remaking you into a vessel that seems best to Him.

DIVINE APPOINTMENTS

My soul thirsts for God, for the living God.
When can I go and meet with God?
Psalm 42:2

Have you ever considered that you have a divine appointment? That when you get up early for your quiet time of prayer and meditation in God's Word, Jesus is waiting to meet with you there?

Have you ever thought of going to church or Bible study as a divine appointment? That Jesus is patiently, personally waiting to meet with you there?

The Samaritan woman had no idea that her trip to the well was a divine appointment. But it was. She found Jesus waiting for her there. Later she invited others to "come, see a man who told me everything I ever did" (John 4:29).

What a difference it would make in our attitude of expectancy and in our habit of consistency in our daily devotions, if we truly wrapped our hearts around the knowledge that it is a divine appointment!

Jesus longs to meet with *you*. Don't keep Him waiting!

YOUR TEARS ARE HIS

When Jesus saw her weeping, and the Jews
who had come along with her also weeping, he
was deeply moved in spirit and troubled.
John 11:33

God so closely identifies with you as His child that your tears are on His face! When God called Abraham to leave Ur of the Chaldeans and follow Him in faith, He encouraged him by promising, "I will bless those who bless you, and whoever curses you I will curse" (Genesis 12:3). God would be so closely identified with Abraham that Abraham's friends and enemies would be His own.

God not only loves His children; He identifies with them. In response to such loyalty and love, we are to identify with Him—with His grief, His joy, His love, His pain, His blessings, His honor, His Son, His gospel. Your pain is His pain. And He loved you enough to send His own Son to identify with your sin and to shed His blood and take your judgment at the cross!

So ... isn't it time His tears were on your face?

HE IS ABLE

Therefore he is able to save completely those
who come to God through him, because he
always lives to intercede for them.
Hebrews 7:25

What problem are you facing today? Maybe it is something in your work? Or is it a marriage that needs reconciling? Or could it be a memory that needs healing? What situation seems impossible to you? God is the God of the impossible! He can make a way where there is no way. God is much bigger than we think. He "is able to do immeasurably more than all we ask or imagine, according to his power that is at work in us" (Ephesians 3:20).

He is able to make all grace abound to you (2 Corinthians 9:8).

He is able to aid those who are tempted (Hebrews 2:18).

He is able to keep you from stumbling (Jude v. 24).

He is able to keep what we have committed to Him until that day (2 Timothy 1:12).

God is more than able to sustain your marriage. He is more than able to work out your finances. To reconcile that relationship. To overcome that disease. He is more than able to solve your problem.

Will you *trust* Him for *every* detail? He is able!

KNOWING GOD AS HE IS

I keep asking that the God of our Lord Jesus Christ,
the glorious Father, may give you the Spirit of wisdom
and revelation, so that you may know him better.
Ephesians 1:17

Are you worshiping a God you've made up? A God who meets your needs—by your own definition? A God who's convenient? A God who bears no resemblance to the God of Abraham, Isaac, and Jacob? I don't want to know God like that. I want to know Him as He is.

I want to know Him like Noah did ... as his salvation from judgment. Like Moses did ... as his liberator from oppression. Like Elijah did ... as his peace in the midst of a whirlwind, earthquake, and fire. Like Jeremiah did ... as One who is faithful and true when his nation was disintegrating.

Jesus prayed, "Now this is eternal life: that they may know you, the only true God, and Jesus Christ, whom you have sent" (John 17:3). Knowing God and bringing Him glory are the reasons for our existence. God knows you. But how well do you know God?

Make it your priority to know God and to grow in your knowledge of Him, so that you know Him better today than yesterday and better tomorrow than today.

JESUS HAS MADE GOD KNOWN

No one has ever seen God, but God the One and Only,
who is at the Father's side, has made him known.
John 1:18

Do you want to *really* know God? How do we take that first step in God's direction? Do we go to church every time the door opens? Or do more good works than bad? Walk barefooted over fiery coals? Pray face-down five times a day?

If we ever truly know God, it will be because He has made Himself available to be known. First John 1:5 says, "This is the message we have heard … and declare to you: God is light." The primary characteristic of light is that it makes itself visible. God has made Himself visible to us in two primary ways. First, He has made Himself visible through Jesus Christ. The second way is through Scripture. He has revealed Himself to us through our Bibles.

If you want to know God, then open your Bible and start reading. Take a good look at Jesus. God is exactly like Him.

SPIRITUAL EYE CHECK

"But seek first his kingdom and his righteousness,
and all these things will be given to you as well."
Matthew 6:33

What's your place of compromise? Did you start out on a journey of authentic faith and then get sidetracked by other desires? More money and things? More popularity and recognition? Other people to impress? Have you sacrificed family or friends so you can be more successful? All of those things are distractions, diversions, detours on your journey of faith.

Jesus said, "Your eye is the lamp of your body. When your eyes are good, your whole body is full of light. But when they are bad, your body also is full of darkness" (Luke 11:34). The *eye* Jesus is referring to is your focus. If your focus is on His kingdom and His righteousness, then your life will be in line with His. But if you compromise, your life gets out of focus. Then the darkness of confusion, fear, and doubt takes over.

So get your spiritual eyes checked, and restart your journey. Refocus on Jesus.

OCTOBER

Every life that would be strong must have its
Holy of Holies into which only God enters.

Mrs. Charles E. Cowman, *Streams in the Desert* (December 4)

AVOID FAILURE

> He restores my soul. He guides me in paths
> of righteousness for his name's sake.
> *Psalm 23:3*

I've never heard of anyone deliberately deciding to fail. People often tell me about their struggles, but no one has ever said, "Today I'm going to fail." We all *do* fail, but I've never met anyone who did it intentionally.

The same is true of *spiritual* failure. It happens to all of us, but where does it begin? For Abraham, it began with a famine of the Word of God and of prayer.

Abraham made a seemingly small, innocent, and practical decision when, according to Genesis 12:10, "There was a famine in the land, and Abram went down to Egypt to live there for a while." There was no prayer, no word from God telling him to go. Totally on his own, Abraham took the first step into drastic failure that would ultimately cause enormous suffering in the lives of others.

What obvious decisions have you made without asking the Lord for guidance? "Trust in the LORD with all your heart and lean not on your own understanding; in all your ways acknowledge him, and he will make your paths straight" (Proverbs 3:5–6).

Avoid failure. Trust and follow Him.

PILLARS IN THE TEMPLE OF GOD

> Him who overcomes I will make a pillar
> in the temple of my God.
> *Revelation 3:12*

The church at Philadelphia was one of the seven churches Jesus addressed in Revelation: "I have placed before you an open door that no one can shut" (3:8). He had set before them an open door for service, and they had walked through it.

As I visited there, I thought of my own life, when I feel inadequate to walk through the doors of opportunity God places before me. How many times over the years I've argued with the Lord.

Not enough time.

Not enough energy.

Not enough education.

And then He'd whisper to my heart, "Anne, walk through that open door. Hold on to what you have: you have Me, and you have the Word of God."

Jesus told the church at Philadelphia He would make them "a pillar in the temple of God." During a trip to the Holy Land, I observed all that was left of the church at Philadelphia and couldn't help but notice—the pillars were still standing!

Get Up ... and Pray

I lie down and sleep; I wake again,
because the LORD sustains me.
Psalm 3:5

Prayer has always been a struggle for me. In fact, I've described it as the fight of my life. One thing is consistent! It's my struggle to maintain a quality time alone with God every day. I have failed more often than I have succeeded. What about you? How's your prayer life? Are you rushing through your prayer time? Neglecting it altogether?

Isaiah 50:4 says, "The Sovereign LORD has given me an instructed tongue, to know the word that sustains the weary. He wakens me morning by morning." When my body wants to roll over and go back to sleep, my spirit says, "Get up, Anne, or you will miss the word God has for you this morning. The very word that will sustain you today, a word for you to share that will sustain someone else."

What blessing are you missing because you're sleeping instead of listening to what God has to say? You'll never know until you get up ... and pray!

"LOVE EACH OTHER!"

"My command is this: Love each other as I have loved you."
John 15:12

J esus couldn't have been clearer when He said to His disciples, "Love each other as I have loved you."

I imagine Peter looking at overly cautious Thomas and wondering, "You mean love *him*, Lord?" Or John gazing at his zealous brother, James, with all their years of sibling rivalry, and thinking, *I've been trying to love him for years. The best I can do is tolerate him!*

In case we forget our Lord's message, He repeated it twice in John 15: "Love each other" (vv. 12, 17). It's a command!

What person are you tolerating instead of loving? Is it because that person grates on your nerves? Instead of avoiding that person, Jesus commands you to love him or her. You'll see that as you obey His command, He'll use that person to grind off your sharp, impatient, un-Christlike edges.

Jesus said, "Love each other." And then He said it again: "Love each other."

NOTHING CAN SEPARATE YOU

If I go up to the heavens, you are there; if I make my bed
in the depths, you are there. If I rise on the wings of the
dawn, if I settle on the far side of the sea, even there your
hand will guide me, your right hand will hold me fast.
Psalm 139:8–10

Jesus is with you now and for all eternity because He lives in you and has promised *nothing* will separate you from Him. There isn't a place in the entire universe where Jesus is not! Romans 8:38–39 confirms this promise: "Neither death nor life, nor angels nor principalities nor powers, nor things present nor things to come, nor height nor depth, nor any other created thing, will be able to separate us from the love of God."

What do you think can separate you from God? A spouse who forsakes you? A boss who fires you? Parents who abandoned you? Failure? Death? The truth is that nothing can separate you from God's love. *Nothing!*

When you're overwhelmed with burdens, God loves you. When adversity increases in intensity, God loves you. When friends forsake you, when enemies attack you, when children rebel against you ... God loves you.

God *really* does love you! If ever you're tempted to doubt it, take a look at His Word. Jesus said, "The Father loves you." Then He stretched out His arms on the cross and proved it.

A SHOWCASE FOR HIS GLORY

> But we have this treasure in jars of clay to show that this all-surpassing power is from God and not from us. We are hard pressed on every side, but not crushed; perplexed, but not in despair; persecuted, but not abandoned; struck down, but not destroyed. We always carry around in our body the death of Jesus, so that the life of Jesus may also be revealed in our body.
>
> *2 Corinthians 4:7–10*

Someone is watching you.

What a sobering thought! Who is watching the way you handle your problems and disputes? Your mate? A child? A co-worker? An employee? A roommate? Often it's someone you don't even know is watching.

One reason God allows us to have problems is so we can demonstrate to a watching world how His children respond to difficulties. First Peter 1:7 says, "These have come so that your faith—of greater worth than gold, which perishes even though refined by fire—may be proved genuine and may result in praise, glory and honor" to God.

Maybe the person who's watching is someone you have talked to about Jesus, and now God is giving you the opportunity to show the difference Jesus can make in everyday life. When that person looks at you, what will he or she see? Be a showcase for God's glory!

GOD IS FOR YOU!

Who will bring any charge against those whom
God has chosen? It is God who justifies.
Romans 8:33

What time is it in your life? Have you been in a battle with the enemy? Have you recently taken a bold step of faith? Could it be that you have followed through with the commitment to let everything go to pursue knowing God and now you are wondering, *What in the world have I done? What is this going to mean?*

Are you suddenly afraid of being too radical, too fanatical in your faith? Are you afraid of the consequences of having done the right thing?

After Abraham defeated a powerful enemy to rescue his nephew Lot, he was terrified of the repercussions. But God spoke to him in Genesis 15:1, "Do not be afraid, Abram. I am your shield, your very great reward."

Don't be afraid. Just do the right thing. God is for you! He's on your side!

WHERE IS THE MAN IN THE GAP?

I looked for a man among them who would build up the
wall and stand before me in the gap on behalf of the land
so I would not have to destroy it, but I found none.
Ezekiel 22:30

What's gone wrong? Why is our nation in such turmoil? Such difficulty? We've experienced financial shortfalls, people losing jobs, losing their homes. People have suffered broken dreams, broken hopes, broken hearts. We blame the economy. Or the politicians. Or poor decisions.

But that's *not* the basic problem. The basic, primary problem is *sin*. And the basic, primary solution is the *Savior*. The time is now to solve the underlying issue by repenting of our sin and turning to God.

The healing of America depends on the cleansing of your heart and mine as we confess and turn away from our sin. God has told us, "If my people, who are called by my name, will humble themselves and pray and seek my face and turn from their wicked ways, then will I hear from heaven and will forgive their sin and will heal their land" (2 Chronicles 7:14).

So what are you waiting for? Get on your knees ... now!

DON'T SETTLE FOR LESS

Praise be to the God and Father of our Lord
Jesus Christ, who has blessed us in the heavenly
realms with every spiritual blessing in Christ.
Ephesians 1:3

What are you settling for in your life? What are you willing to compromise for comfort? Happiness? Prestige or wealth?

It's far too easy to settle for less. Less than the fullness of God's blessing. Less than God's purpose for your life. And soon what matters to others seems more important than what matters to God.

Surfing the Internet becomes more important than reading your Bible. Going to the gym seems more important than early-morning prayer time.

Jesus opened His heart to His Father and prayed, "And now, Father, glorify me in your presence with the glory I had with you before the world began" (John 17:5). Jesus was asking His Father to give Him *more*! *More* glory! *More* blessing!

Don't settle for less than everything God wants to give you.

THIRSTY FOR GOD

"Salt is good, but if it loses its saltiness, how can
you make it salty again? Have salt in yourselves,
and be at peace with each other."
Mark 9:50

Our culture seems to elevate toleration, inclusiveness, and political correctness to the extreme. And the culture in which we live seems to be infecting Christians.

When Jesus said, "Love each another" (John 15:12), He didn't mean we should tolerate sin. When Jesus said, "Do not judge, or you too will be judged" (Matthew 7:1), He didn't mean we are not to recognize and take a stand against sinful behavior.

Don't misunderstand what He is saying, or you are running the risk of hiding the light of truth under a bushel basket of cultural defects. The saltiness of your life will be lost and will no longer hinder the corruption around you.

Be the light of the truth that stands out in the darkness of a culture of compromise and spin. Be a salty saint who makes people thirsty for God.

LIFE STORMS

Then the LORD spoke to Job out of the storm.
Job 40:6

E very day we hear of devastation from environmental storms, hurricanes, and earthquakes. We also experience personal storms that are just as devastating yet not as obvious: Your company downsizes, and your job is gone. A child gets sick. Elderly parents need you more than ever. Relationships are strained.

I can tell you my own family hasn't been exempt from those storms that come to discourage and cause us to lose hope.

When the prophet Isaiah experienced the storm of King Uzziah's death, he testified, "I saw the Lord" (Isaiah 6:1). Isaiah raised his eyes to God for a fresh vision of God's purpose in his life, for His presence, peace, and power.

What storm has struck your life? Don't look back or around or ahead. Look *up*! Ask God to give you a fresh vision of Jesus. Ask Him to speak to you in the midst of the storm. Then ask Him to give you a renewed passion to tell others about Him.

DON'T WASTE YOUR WILDERNESS

My times are in your hands.
Psalm 31:15

God's time is perfect. But so often it's not *our* perfect time, is it?
I remember how, when my children were small, I felt bound by smallness—clothes, toys, sticky fingerprints, small talk. While I'm convinced nothing is as significant as rearing godly children, I believed life held more.

My wise mother said, "Anne, don't waste your wilderness years." She said if one day God called me to serve Him outside my home, I needed to be ready. So, I disciplined myself to pray and study my Bible on a daily basis.

I was encouraged by Hosea 2:14, where God promised He would "speak tenderly" to me in the wilderness. And He did. Years later, when God called me out into the world, I was ready.

What about you? What are you doing today to prepare for serving God tomorrow—or whenever He calls you? Remember my mother's wisdom. Don't waste your wilderness years!

GOD IS WITH YOU!

> The LORD Almighty is with us; the
> God of Jacob is our fortress.
> *Psalm 46:7*

Have you said to God, "If You really loved me, You'd heal me"? "If You really loved me, You would have prevented my spouse from leaving"? "If You really loved me, I'd still have my job"? God has *proved* His love for us, once and forever, at the cross. Romans 5:8 reminds us, "God demonstrates His love for us in this: While we were still sinners, Christ died for us."

When bad things happen to those God loves, the wonderful promise is that He will be with us in the midst of those bad things. He promises that when the worst happens, even when you face death, He will be with you (Psalm 23:4). God promises, "When you pass through the waters, I will be with you" (Isaiah 43:2). And He promises, "Never will I leave you; never will I forsake you" (Hebrews 13:5).

He is with you. Stop complaining—and start claiming God's promise.

PEACE DANCING

"If you obey my commands, you will remain in my
love, just as I have obeyed my Father's commands and
remain in his love. I have told you this so that my joy
may be in you and that your joy may be complete."
John 15:10–11

Joy is supremely different from happiness. *Happiness,* considered our "inalienable right" as Americans, depends on circumstances or things or people or feelings. But *joy* is something else. I like the definition that joy is "peace dancing." Joy is rooted in a deep contentment that is independent of everything—except our relationship with God.

In our relationship with Him, we find all that brings "sparkle" to life:

Joy!

Love.

Satisfaction and a sense of fulfillment.

Purpose.

Hope.

Jesus said He told us these things so our joy would be complete.

Do you lack joy because you don't know the things He has told you? Then start reading your Bible. Enjoy life today!

HEAR HIM SPEAK TO YOU

The law from your mouth is more precious to me
than thousands of pieces of silver and gold.
Psalm 119:72

When you're confused about what God is saying to you, open your Bible and *listen* as you read! Several years ago, as I prepared messages for a leadership seminar in a mountain retreat, my preparation wasn't going well. I struggled through the material, feeling very inadequate and overwhelmed.

But then God spoke to me from Isaiah 25:6: "On this mountain the Lord Almighty will prepare a feast of rich food for all peoples." As I claimed His promise to me, I was strengthened and encouraged. And I had the absolute joy of watching Him turn my feeble preparation into a "rich feast" for everyone who came.

God knows what's going on in your life, and He will speak to you through His Word. But how will you know what He has to say if you don't open your Bible and read it? Don't miss His encouragement. Hear Him speak to you. Read your Bible today.

SLEEP IN PEACE

I will lie down and sleep in peace, for you
alone, O Lord, make me dwell in safety.
Psalm 4:8

Are you without peace? Apprehensive? Even afraid? God gives you and me promises that bring peace in the midst of panic. But we have to tune our hearts to listen to His voice—as the psalmist advised, "Great peace have they who love your law" (Psalm 119:165).

One of the first verses I memorized was stored away in my mind because I'm such a worrier: "Do not be anxious about anything, but in everything, by prayer and petition, with thanksgiving, present your requests to God. And the peace of God, which transcends all understanding, will guard your hearts and your minds in Christ Jesus" (Philippians 4:6–7). Prayerful focus on God and His promises has brought me peace when I've been worried.

God understands your fears, your anxieties. So tell Him about them and then rest in Him as you leave your worries with Him.

RIVETED ON HIM

When Jacob awoke from his sleep, he thought, "Surely
the LORD is in this place, and I was not aware of it."
Genesis 28:16

For me, the journey of obedient faith has, at times, been like a long walk in the same direction—with *nobody*! It can be very lonely.

Maybe you're feeling lonely in your faith walk right now. Are you recently divorced, and you've discovered you're vulnerable to the self-righteous criticism of others?

Have you decided to go back to work, opening yourself to attacks from friends who feel your place is in the home?

Have you taken a bold stand for the truth of God's Word, knowing you'll be accused of being narrow-minded?

God is there beside you as your shield, your hiding place, your stronghold. He understands how it feels to be alone, facing attack.

The Bible tells us when tension surrounds us to "be still, and know that I am God" (Psalm 46:10). Center down on Him. Take a few moments to be quiet. Make a list of at least ten of God's attributes and focus on them. Then talk to Him about who He is.

God is there with you. And He is a majority of One!

TAKE GOD AT HIS WORD

All these people were still living by faith when they
died. They did not receive the things promised; they
only saw them and welcomed them from a distance....
Instead, they were longing for a better country—a
heavenly one. Therefore God is not ashamed to be
called their God, for he has prepared a city for them.

Hebrews 11:13, 16

Have you taken God at His Word, but He hasn't come through for you? Have you poured out your heart to God about your spouse who's ill but doesn't seem to get better? A rebellious child who still refuses to obey? A boss whose demands have become even more unreasonable?

Is this situation creating an opening for doubt about your beliefs? When a father brought his troubled son to Jesus, he said, "I do believe; help me overcome my unbelief!" (Mark 9:24). Sometimes we need help to trust God completely. If you're still waiting for God to fulfill His promise to you, if you're beginning to doubt He'll really answer, ask Him to give you another promise from His Word to confirm the original one.

Like the people of Hebrews 11 who have gone before us, we need to just take Him at His Word. Believe it!

Believe *Him*!

HE GIVES ALL THINGS

Your word, O LORD, is eternal; it stands firm in the heavens.
Psalm 119:89

Can I know for sure that God has forgiven me of my sin? Can I know He's placed His Holy Spirit in me? Can I know He's given me eternal life? Can I know He's even now preparing a heavenly home for me? Yes! Yes! Yes! I can. I can know for sure, and so can you.

Your hope is secure because God has given you His Word, and then He made a covenant with you. The covenant wasn't sealed with pieces of animals, as in Old Testament days, but with the broken body and shed blood of His own dear Son. You didn't do anything to earn it; therefore, you can't do anything to lose it.

We can believe it because the Bible says it's true: "He who did not spare his own Son, but gave him up for us all—how will he not also ... graciously give us all things?" (Romans 8:32).

God's blessings—forgiveness, eternal life, heaven—do not depend on your word. They depend on His. Take God at His Word!

REAL HAPPINESS

Blessed is he whose transgressions are forgiven, whose sins
are covered. Blessed is the man whose sin the LORD does
not count against him and in whose spirit is no deceit.
Psalm 32:1–2

Unconfessed sin in our lives is one of the greatest barriers to happiness. So before we can be truly happy, we must be cleansed of sin. Before we can be cleansed, we must confess our sin. Before we can confess it, we must be convicted of sin.

When Jesus searches *your* life, what does He find?

Will you say, with the psalmist, "Search me, O God, and know my heart … See if there is any offensive way in me" (Psalm 139:23–24)? The good news is that when Jesus searches us, when He finds and convicts us of sin, He doesn't leave us there. God's Word also tells us, "If we confess our sins, he is faithful and just and will forgive us our sins and purify us from all unrighteousness" (1 John 1:9). *All* unrighteousness.

Invite Jesus to search your heart. Confess your sin. Ask for cleansing. Then be prepared to experience real happiness!

LOOK TO JESUS

When I am afraid, I will trust in you.

Psalm 56:3

We all have sleepless nights, don't we? Tossing and turning. Looking at the clock and seeing it's barely moved. Stressing because we know we need to sleep if we're going to make it through the next day.

How often do you lie there anxious about situations you can't do anything about? Jesus tells us, "Do not let your hearts be troubled. Trust in God; trust also in me" (John 14:1). The answer to fear ... is faith. When you're fearful for a loved one or fearful about some event coming up in your life, you can be comforted and calmed as you think about who God is. Then, as you focus on the attributes of God, your faith is planted in Someone bigger than your fears.

The next time fear overwhelms you, look for a Scripture verse that underscores God's character. And consider who He is. Don't look to your problem. Look to Jesus!

WHEN GOD IS PLEASED

So we make it our goal to please him.
2 Corinthians 5:9

Have you ever wondered if Jesus was tempted to doubt whether He had pleased God with His life and ministry? Could Satan have tempted Him to have the fleeting thought that the cross was evidence God was *not* pleased?

We know Jesus had *no doubt* that His Father was pleased, because God leaned out of heaven and said, "You are my Son, whom I love; with you I am well pleased" (Luke 3:22).

Recently someone remarked, "Anne, I know God is pleased with you." But I was left to wonder how that person knew. Was it just a feeling?

How can anyone know when God is pleased? Do we assume He is pleased when we enjoy good health? When our job is going well? When our investments yield a significant return? When people speak well of us? When our prayers are answered? When we're happy?

On what do we base the evidence of His favor and goodwill?

But then I knew. It's His Word that tells me what pleases Him. I don't have to be left wondering, doubting, or fearing that I'm not pleasing to Him. I just need to open my Bible, read, apply, and obey it. He will be pleased.

GOD'S GRACE IS SUFFICIENT

*From the fullness of his grace we have all received one
blessing after another. For the law was given through
Moses; grace and truth came through Jesus Christ.*
John 1:16–17

When was your last attack of the "if onlys"? Thinking about what might have been can send you into a downward spiral of depression, can't it? There have been dreadful times in my life when I have wrestled with deep regret to the point that I have cried out with weeping, "If only …!" I had to take all of those painful regrets to the foot of the cross and leave them there. I had to lay myself down in God's grace and plead for His mercy to break the emotional and spiritual paralysis the "if onlys" had caused.

Stop living in the past. That was then. The apostle Paul reminded us that Jesus has promised, "My grace is sufficient for you" (2 Corinthians 12:9). God's grace is sufficient to cover the "if onlys." He will give you a fresh start.

Stop looking in the rearview mirror and start looking forward!

LIVE A FULL LIFE

"I have come that they may have life, and have it to the full."
John 10:10

How fully will you live out your life? To live life as Jesus created it involves developing a personal relationship with Him. It involves talking with Him in prayer. It involves listening to Him as you read God's Word … and then applying what God says to your life.

If it's a promise, claim it. If it's a command, obey it. If it's encouragement, accept it. If it's a warning, heed it. Jesus said, "I am the vine; you are the branches. If a man remains in me and I in him, he will bear much fruit; apart from me you can do nothing" (John 15:5).

Don't stop short of living the abundant life Jesus has promised believers … a life that is eternally significant, a life that brings glory to God. Be consistent. Be obedient. Be dependent. Live a full life!

THE PEAK OF GOD'S POWER

But he said to me, "My grace is sufficient for you,
for my power is made perfect in weakness."
2 Corinthians 12:9

Have you ever suffered from the same thing for a long time? Have you prayed repeatedly for God to take whatever it is from you, but He has seemed to remain silent and still? Or perhaps He has given you many promises regarding your situation, but yet none have been fulfilled? The apostle Paul experienced a similar issue. He had what he called a thorn in his flesh, a messenger of Satan, that tormented him. We sometimes think of it as a rose thorn or a splinter, when in actual fact he was describing a nail that was impaling him. Three times he earnestly prayed for it to be taken away . . . and Paul was someone who knew how to get answers to his prayers. However, the Lord responded: "My grace is sufficient for you, for my power is made perfect in weakness."

Like Paul, as I look back on my life, I have found that the most difficult and painful situations have also been the times when I have experienced God's strength and peace on a supernatural level. The "thorns" that pinned Him to the cross have pressed me closer to Himself. So, I pray for deliverance. But if He says no, I embrace the pain, knowing it will vault me to the pinnacles of His power.

A PLUMB LINE

Oh, how I love your law! I meditate on it all
day long. Your commands make me wiser than
my enemies, for they are ever with me.
Psalm 119:97–98

Have you ever hung wallpaper and just guessed that you were hanging it straight? I have—and it was a disaster! I learned the hard way that I should have used a plumb line, because wallpaper can look straight yet be very crooked.

As we look at the way we live our lives, things can seem fairly straight. We compare ourselves with each other and adjust our values to fit the norm. And before we realize it, we're in a crooked, mismatched mess.

God asked the prophet Amos, "What do you see, Amos?" And he replied, "A plumb line" (Amos 7:8). God then indicated that His Word is like a plumb line. Without it, we're just guessing, hoping we'll get it right. God's Word tells us what is right and wrong, what is pleasing to God and what is not.

Don't just stumble along. Use God's plumb line. Read the Word!

LIVING IN HIS PRESENCE

As they approached the village to which they were going,
Jesus acted as if he were going farther. But they urged
him strongly, "Stay with us, for it is nearly evening; the
day is almost over." So he went in to stay with them.
Luke 24:28–29

What blessings of God do we miss when we rush away from His presence?

When I've hurried through my prayer time, jumped up off my knees, quickly shut my Bible, closed my notebook, and hurried off to take on my day, I've thought of the disciples on the Emmaus Road who longed to linger in God's presence.

I wonder! Has God wanted to reveal Himself to me in a way I've never seen before, but I didn't have time to *linger*? Do *you* rush through your time with God too? Let's slow down. Let's keep our eyes closed, our heads bowed for just a few minutes longer, and reflect on the Scripture reading for just one more moment. Will we hear God whisper?

James 4:8 says, "Come near to God and he will come near to *you*" (emphasis mine). Listen! I think I hear Him coming now ...

FEEDING OTHERS WITH LITTLE BITS

When they had finished eating, Jesus said to Simon
Peter, "Simon son of John, do you truly love me
more than these?" "Yes, Lord," he said, "you know
that I love you." Jesus said, "Feed my lambs."
John 21:15

D o you think God can't use you because you can offer Him only a little
bit of time, a little bit of money, a little bit of knowledge? Remember
that Jesus can make a little bit … more than enough.

When Jesus and His disciples set aside time for a retreat, five thousand
people showed up. They wanted Jesus to heal them and teach them. But
apparently none of them brought a thing to eat.

The disciples tried to persuade Jesus to "send the crowd away." But Jesus
said, "You give them something to eat." So Andrew found a little boy with
five loaves and two fish … just little bits of food. Then, "taking the five
loaves and the two fish and looking up to heaven, he gave thanks and broke
them. Then he gave them to the disciples to set before the people." All five
thousand were fed (Luke 9:12–13, 16–17).

Jesus can use broken pieces. He can take a little bit and make it *more*
than enough!

LOVE AS HE LOVES YOU

This is how we know what love is: Jesus Christ
laid down his life for us. And we ought to
lay down our lives for our brothers.
1 John 3:16

Who do you know who goes against your grain? Who is the one you always seem to clash with? The person you are incompatible with? Is it your boss? A neighbor? Your spouse? A teenage child? You can't avoid the person because you live or work with him or her, and the clash is always there. Maybe the relationship has become so strained it feels like the person is an enemy.

Jesus gives you and me a different approach. A new way: *His* way. The key that enables us to love our enemies—to love anyone we are incompatible with—comes in Jesus' words: "My command is this: Love each other as I have loved you" (John 15:12). A few verses later, He repeats the command: "Love each other!" (John 15:17).

Make your relationship with Jesus the priority. Then love others sacrificially—unconditionally—as He has loved you!

GOD KNOWS YOU

O LORD, you have searched me and you know
me. You know when I sit and when I rise;
you perceive my thoughts from afar.
Psalm 139:1–2

What is unspoken in your life? Something you feel you are not able to share with anyone? Is it loneliness? Or isolation? That sense of not being connected? Or that longing for someone who would understand? Someone who would know how you are feeling without your having to say a word?

We all long for someone like that at one time or another. And Jesus is that person! He *knows*. Everything! The unspoken questions on your mind. The unexpressed feelings in your heart. He understands.

Psalm 139:3–4 says, "You discern my going out and my lying down; you are familiar with all my ways. Before a word is on my tongue you know it completely, O LORD." When you feel lonely, isolated, disconnected . . . when you need your questions answered, turn to the One who is totally familiar with all your ways . . . and with you!

YOUR ALARM CLOCK

Let us draw near to God with a sincere heart in
full assurance of faith, having our hearts sprinkled
to cleanse us from a guilty conscience and
having our bodies washed with pure water.
Hebrews 10:22

Guilt is not something you should ignore, not something you should drug or drown or excuse. Guilt is your friend.

Does that surprise you? Guilt is like an alarm clock, your wake-up call! If you rationalize your guilt or drown it in alcohol or bury it in work, you risk exposing yourself to God's judgment.

Jesus says the Holy Spirit "will convict the world of guilt" (John 16:8). The conviction of sin and that guilty feeling should drive us to the cross in confession of sin, so that we might be cleansed ... and our guilt can be removed. There is only one stain remover for the guilt of sin, and it's the blood of Jesus. Let your guilt drive you to the cross. Then you will experience the cleansing flow of the blood that washes white as snow.

So when the alarm goes off, pay attention!

NOVEMBER

Amidst my list of blessings infinite
Stands this the foremost, that my heart has bled;
For all I bless Thee, most for the severe.

Hugh Macmillan, quoted in
Mrs. Charles E. Cowman, *Streams in the Desert* (October 1)

JUST A PRAYER AWAY

May your unfailing love be my comfort,
according to your promise to your servant.
Psalm 119:76

Loneliness isn't just being alone—it's isolation. Separation. Not feeling connected. We've all experienced it. Perhaps right now you're longing for someone who'd understand you to such depth that he or she would know how you're feeling without your having to say a word. Someone who'd tenderly look into your eyes, and you would know that person knew ... everything!

Jesus is that Someone! He knows the unspoken questions on your mind and the unexpressed feelings in your heart. He knows, and He understands!

God said to the prophet Isaiah, "As a mother comforts her child, so will I comfort you; and you will be comforted" (Isaiah 66:13). As a child of God, the Holy Spirit is Jesus in you, giving all of Himself to you!

When you feel lonely.

When you need your questions answered.

When you feel like talking, but there's no one you trust.

Go to Jesus. He's just a prayer away.

Pray Continually

Be joyful always; pray continually; give thanks in all
circumstances, for this is God's will for you in Christ Jesus.
1 Thessalonians 5:16–18

Have you prayed for someone "continually," as the Bible commands, and yet you've seen no evidence of God's activity in that person's life? Have you concluded God hasn't heard your prayers? Or that He doesn't care?

God doesn't always act according to our timetable. He's very patient. But never mistake His patience for inactivity. Sometimes God will test and strengthen your faith by withholding evidence of His working, so that your faith is in Him alone. But God is faithful.

Jesus asked Martha, "Did I not tell you that if you believed, you would see the glory of God?" (John 11:40).

When she saw no evidence of God's activity, He was still at work. He raised her brother from the dead!

God is active whether or not you and I can see evidence of it. Listen to me! Believe in Jesus! He is active. You will see the glory!

HIDDEN AGENDAS?

Whether you eat or drink or whatever you
do, do it all for the glory of God.
1 Corinthians 10:31

What are the hidden agendas in your prayers? We all have them—we just don't like to own up to them!

Are you praying for God to save your marriage to avoid being humiliated?

Are you afraid for your reputation if your children don't succeed on schedule?

Are you asking for financial relief because you're tired of budgeting?

So many of our requests are rooted in selfishness and pride. But Jesus understands those feelings. He knows our need to feel worthwhile, but glorifying God should be our bottom-line agenda.

So … feel free to ask God whatever you want … to do whatever you want … to say whatever you want. Just make sure it's all ultimately for His glory.

YOUR HELPER

Cast all your anxiety on him because he cares for you.
1 Peter 5:7

Your toddler has spilled his third glass of milk—in the last hour! Your six-year-old is coming down with the flu, and you're just trying to stay on top of what already seems like an impossible day.

I know. I've been there. But when we're totally helpless, God is a God of the impossible! He is your helper. The friend you can turn to. Your counselor.

We can be so foolish at times! Why do we think God isn't interested in our feelings? In our stress? In our day? Nothing is too mundane for your heavenly Father. There's nothing you can hide from God's loving compassion. Tell Him about your stress, your frustration.

God cares about what you care about ... because He cares for you.

JUST ASK

This is the confidence we have in approaching God:
that if we ask anything according to his will, he hears
us. And if we know that he hears us—whatever we
ask—we know that we have what we asked of him.
1 John 5:14–15

My mother once said if there are any tears shed in heaven, they're going to be shed over all the answers to prayer for which no one ever bothered to ask! John 16:23 quotes Jesus, who said, "I tell you the truth, my Father will give you whatever you ask in my name."

To ask and pray in Jesus' name means you come to God believing that Jesus is your Lord and Savior—believing He died and rose for you, and in response you have submitted to His authority. Jesus is waiting for you to ask! Waiting because He wants to get your attention. He wants you to acknowledge your need of Him. And when the answer comes, you will know it comes from Him.

Ask according to God's will. Ask in Jesus' name. Just ask.

LASTING CHANGE

Therefore, if anyone is in Christ, he is a new
creation; the old has gone, the new has come!
2 Corinthians 5:17

The older I get, the more I want things to be comfortable, familiar: the same styles, the same restaurants, even the same seat in church. Change can be unsettling, and it requires energy I don't always have. So I don't want change just for the sake of change.

But I also never want to get to the place where I refuse to step out of the boat—and miss the thrill of walking on the water. What I do want is a good reason for change; I want assurance that the change will bring something better. Like the change that occurs when the gospel is preached and a change occurs in our hearts that reconciles us to God through faith in Christ Jesus. The change Jesus meant when He said, "To all who received him, he gave the right to become children of God" (John 1:12).

Celebrate the best kind of change—*lasting* change and *living* hope—in Jesus Christ!

LIGHT IN A DARK WORLD

"This is the verdict: Light has come into the world, but men
loved darkness instead of light because their deeds were evil."
John 3:19

There may be good reasons why your old friends avoid you. Why co-workers keep their distance. Why your neighbors would rather not get too close. John 1:5 says, "The light shines in the darkness, but the darkness has not understood it."

When you live a life that reflects Jesus, His light reveals the rebellion and ignorance in the world. If your friends or co-workers or neighbors are living in darkness, the Light in you makes them uncomfortable. They may think they're getting along perfectly okay on their own. But the light of your life may make them realize they're *not* doing okay.

When you live a life that reflects God's integrity and morality and purity, His holiness and righteousness and truthfulness, His goodness and godliness and grace—the light can be blinding. It can cause others to react with rejection.

Be encouraged. That same Light that reveals the darkness—*also reigns over it*! So . . . turn on the Light!

SET YOUR COMPASS

Very early in the morning, while it was still
dark, Jesus got up, left the house and went
off to a solitary place, where he prayed.
Mark 1:35

Jesus invites us to draw aside and spend time with Him. Why don't we? We need to *have* time to spend time. And I don't have any to spend! So the bottom line is that it's up to me to *make* the time. If I'm not careful, I will succumb to the tyranny of the urgent and miss those moments of divine encounter.

So here's my simple solution: I make sure that at least once a day, I intentionally draw aside with Jesus. It's like setting my spiritual compass. John said that "our fellowship is with the Father and with his Son, Jesus Christ … to make our joy complete" (1 John 1:3–4).

If you're bombarded by pressures, problems, and unwelcome news … if your spirit is overwhelmed and your joy is incomplete … if you long for intimate fellowship with Jesus, then make time for Him.

LOVE COVERS

*Above all, love each other deeply, because
love covers over a multitude of sins.*

1 Peter 4:8

King Solomon in his wisdom said, "He who covers over an offense promotes love, but whoever repeats the matter separates close friends" (Proverbs 17:9). One definition of love is in 1 Corinthians 13:6–7: "Love does not delight in evil.... It *always* protects" (italics mine).

Peter was one of the greatest failures recorded in the Bible. His most notorious moment of sin came after he vowed that he would die for Jesus, but instead actually denied ever knowing Him—and not just once, but three times. Yet when Peter repented, Jesus restored him so completely he was given a prominent leadership position in the early church. The church forgave Peter and accepted his leadership.

Who do you know who has sinned? Who has denied Jesus by his or her words or behavior? Has that person repented? If so, then you need to extend grace and help restore him or her.

First Corinthians also says love "keeps no record of wrongs" (13:5). Whose sin are you *repeating*—instead of *restoring* the sinner? Instead of commenting on the sin, cover it with God's love and grace.

His Faithful Servant

*Therefore, I urge you, brothers, in view of God's
mercy, to offer your bodies as living sacrifices, holy and
pleasing to God—this is your spiritual act of worship.*
Romans 12:1

What are you doing to meet the needs of others? What are you doing to serve others? Romans 14:18 says, "Anyone who serves Christ in this way is pleasing to God." We should never forget who Jesus is. He is Lord.

And we should never forget who *we* are: His servants. Servants who are sinners who have been saved, blood-bought; servants who are prisoners-freed and glory-bound.

The Bible tells us, "You are not your own; you were bought at a price. Therefore honor God with your body" (1 Corinthians 6:19–20). What does that mean? It means I am to live for what He wants, rather than for what I want. And God wants me to serve others.

You were bought with a price too. You are not your own. So would you choose today to serve Him by serving others?

FREE AT LAST!

So I find this law at work: When I want to do good,
evil is right there with me. For in my inner being I
delight in God's law; but I see another law at work in
the members of my body, waging war against the law
of my mind and making me a prisoner of the law of sin
at work within my members. What a wretched man
I am! Who will rescue me from this body of death?
Thanks be to God—through Jesus Christ our Lord!

Romans 7:21–25

Do you ever get frustrated with the sin in your life? I sure do. Even though I've received forgiveness for all my sin, I still sin. I don't want to. I try not to. I hate sin. But I look forward with hope because one day, when I get to our Father's house, all my sin—my sinful tendencies, thoughts, actions, words, feelings—*all* my sins are going to fall away like a stinking garment that finally is discarded.

First John 3:2 promises, "We know that when he appears, we shall be like him, for we shall see him as he is." No more dirty garments on that day. What will be left is the character of Christ formed in me. I will be like Jesus!

Praise God! I will be free from the struggle with sin. I will be free at last!

GOD IS ALL MIGHTY

The LORD appeared to him [Abraham] and said, "I am
God Almighty; walk before me and be blameless."
Genesis 17:1

Who or what seems to be greater than God? God is not one of "several" gods—a trendy thought these days. Just as a potter is greater than the clay or an artist is greater than his painting, God is greater than His creation.

There's nothing in my life or in yours—no circumstance or crisis, no habit or heartache, no sickness or grief, nothing visible or invisible—nothing that's greater than God! "Through him all things were made; without him nothing was made that has been made" (John 1:3). No king or ruler, no preacher or teacher—no one is greater than God.

What are you facing that's greater than you are? A habit? A person? A problem? Something beyond your ability to handle? God is greater!

Put your focus and your faith in the One who has authority over everything!

EFFECTIVE MESSENGERS

He will bring you a message through which
you and all your household will be saved.

Acts 11:14

D uring political election cycles and commercial breaks on television, we are bombarded by messages at every level. Marketing experts and public relation specialists coach their clients and refine the messages to communicate effectively to masses of people.

In listening to some of the evaluations, we hear a variety of comments like, "They have no message" or "Their message is not clear" or "They use talking points that they circulate to all of their spokespeople to make sure their message gets out" or "He stayed on message" or "They are very effective in getting their message out" or "Now, that was great! They got everyone to talk about …"

The buzz about the messages and the messengers has caused me to pause and think. I know God has a message He wants to get out to the people. Do you and I know what His message is? Have we read His "talking points"? How closely do we follow them? Are we effective messengers for Him? Romans 10:17 explains, "Faith comes from hearing the message, and the message is heard through the word of Christ."

Make it your goal to be an effective messenger of the gospel. Someone's faith in Jesus depends on it.

HEARTS CAN CHANGE

"But I tell you the truth: It is for your good that I
am going away. Unless I go away, the Counselor will
not come to you; but if I go, I will send him to you.
When he comes, he will convict the world of guilt in
regard to sin and righteousness and judgment."

John 16:7–8

I s there someone you've dropped off your prayer list as hopeless to ever
believe in Jesus? Then be encouraged: hearts *can* change!

Nebuchadnezzar was king of the greatest empire in the world. He was
also one of the evilest tyrants in human history, later emulated by the late
Saddam Hussein. Yet his heart was changed through the witness of a young
man who, under God's direction, interpreted his dreams.

The prophet Daniel recorded Nebuchadnezzar's transformation as a
testimony, not only to the world of his day, but to generations that followed.
In Nebuchadnezzar's words, "I praised the Most High; I honored and glorified him who lives forever" (Daniel 4:34). If God could change a most
evil Nebuchadnezzar from the inside out, why do you think He could not
change the person you're praying for?

God has power to change the hardest hearts! Persevere in prayer! For
your Nebuchadnezzar!

HE SATISFIES YOUR DESIRES

O Lord, you have searched me and you know
me. You know when I sit and when I rise;
you perceive my thoughts from afar.
Psalm 139:1–2

Is the desire of your heart to be married? Are you wondering if God knows ... or cares? In the beginning, Adam was single too. And he longed for a companion to share his life. I wonder if he was praying that God would somehow take away the strange ache in his heart and the loneliness he felt inside—especially when he observed that every animal had a mate except him.

Then, while Adam was sleeping, God "took one of the man's ribs and closed up the place with flesh. Then the Lord God made a woman from the rib he had taken out of the man, and he brought her to the man" (Genesis 2:21–22). God knew the desires of Adam's heart. And He knew exactly how to meet them.

And God knows how to meet your emotional needs and satisfy your desires too. Learn a lesson from Adam. Trust God. Just go to sleep in His will.

DISCOVER HIS POWER

For this reason, since the day we heard about you, we have
not stopped praying for you and asking God to fill you with
the knowledge of his will through all spiritual wisdom and
understanding, ... being strengthened with all power according to his
glorious might so that you may have great endurance and patience.

Colossians 1:9, 11

What problem are you facing that feels overwhelming? A lawsuit? A
broken marriage? A wayward child? A loved one who's dying? Elderly
parents who are becoming senile?

Praise God for the omnipotence of Jesus Christ and His all-knowing
power! He is the Almighty—mightier than all. Greater, more powerful,
than any problem or situation you or I will ever face. And His power is
available to you and me.

This is the same "incomparably great power" that "raised [Christ] from
the dead and seated him ... at [God's] right hand" (Ephesians 1:19–20). One
reason God allows us to have problems and be in situations that seem bigger than we are is so we can discover His "incomparably great power." If
our lives are easy, how will we ever experience His power?

When you're in over your head, when there's no way out—get ready to
discover His power!

THE REAL THING

> The true light that gives light to every
> man was coming into the world.
> *John 1:9*

Our world is cluttered with lies, deceit, hypocrisy, and fraud at almost every level. From government leaders to advertisers to business associates, to friends and neighbors—everyone seems to spin the truth.

This "whatever works is right" attitude has crept even into the church. We focus on methods instead of missions, programs instead of prayer. Preachers preach to be popular instead of preaching to change lives. And this shift of focus twists our perception of who Jesus is. Some have sentimentalized Him to the point He's barely recognizable.

If you want to know the truth, saturate yourself in the Word of God, which says, "In the beginning was the Word, and the Word was with God, and the Word was God" (John 1:1). And focus on Jesus' words: "I am ... the truth" (John 14:6).

Shine the light of God's Word on your life. Immerse yourself in Jesus!

You're Equipped

It was he who gave some to be apostles, some to be
prophets, some to be evangelists, and some to be pastors
and teachers, to prepare God's people for works of
service, so that the body of Christ may be built up.
Ephesians 4:11–12

W hat God commands you and me to do, He equips us for. It's that
simple. He's given us the gifts that are necessary to follow Him in
obedience.

Paul said, "There are different kinds of gifts, but the same Spirit. There
are different kinds of service, but the same Lord" (1 Corinthians 12:4–5). If
you want to discover your spiritual gifts, start obeying God.

To say, "I can't obey Him," is invalid. He will never command you to do
something He hasn't equipped and empowered you to do. And if you lack
any gifts, God will bring people alongside you who have the gifts you don't.
That's the body of Christ, each person obeying his or her call, exercising the
particular gifts the Spirit has given. Working together, you'll accomplish
the task to the glory of God.

It's time to get to work. Maybe you can't, but He can! You're *equipped*
by God's Spirit!

Enjoy Your Service

*And we pray this in order that you may live a life worthy of the Lord
and may please him in every way: bearing fruit in every good work,
growing in the knowledge of God, being strengthened with all power
according to his glorious might so that you may have great endurance
and patience, and joyfully giving thanks to the Father, who has qualified
you to share in the inheritance of the saints in the kingdom of light.*
Colossians 1:10–12

What task has God assigned you? Is it to strengthen a marriage, serve a church, teach in a classroom, comfort in a sick room? Do you grumble or complain about the challenge you're facing? Do you neglect or ignore it? Do you resent or resist it?

Paul said, "God loves a cheerful giver" (2 Corinthians 9:7). God wants you and me to enjoy the service we give Him, whatever it may be. Discuss each detail with Him as you do the work.

One of life's greatest pleasures is the joy of working together with God as you complete your work. Often the more difficult the task, the greater the joy because it enables us to see the power of God. He enables us to experience what He can do in and through us—that which we could never do on our own.

Stop procrastinating and start obeying … cheerfully!

GO HOME

So he got up and went to his father. But while he
was still a long way off, his father saw him and was
filled with compassion for him; he ran to his son,
threw his arms around him and kissed him.
Luke 15:20

Are you holding back? Refusing to respond to God? Your heavenly Father has been waiting for you to come home to Him, waiting to celebrate the joy and love and pleasure He wants you to have in relationship with Him. Don't make excuses; don't rationalize your bitterness.

Go to God. Ask Him to cleanse you of your sin. Be courageous and transparent. Ask Him to uproot your bitterness. Ask Him to take control of everything, including past memories of abandonment or abuse or adultery as well as future dreams and disappointments.

Psalm 32:1 says, "Blessed is he whose transgressions are forgiven, whose sins are covered." What blessing are you missing because you're clinging to your sin? Let it go … lay it down at the foot of the cross. Run home to your Father!

CRY OUT

Then they cried out to the LORD in their trouble,
and he delivered them from their distress.
Psalm 107:6

Are you shouting in your spirit, "God, why did You let this thing happen?" Are you defiantly standing in the middle of a mess, yelling in your spirit? Or are you perhaps doing just the opposite, withdrawing in denial and depression, hoping things won't get any worse?

What mess could be worse than the horror of finding yourself in the stinking, slimy insides of a giant fish? I can't imagine a more devastating situation, yet Jonah, in his hopelessness, prayed in just that place: "In my distress I called to the LORD, and he answered me. From the depths of the grave I called for help, and you listened to my cry" (Jonah 2:2).

God heard Jonah's cry. He answered Jonah's prayer and delivered him from his distress.

If God did that for Jonah, will He not do it for you? You won't know until you cry out to Him.

WHEN GOD IS SILENT

Do not hide your face from me when I am in distress.
Turn your ear to me; when I call, answer me quickly.
Psalm 102:2

I s God silent in your life? If He is, could it be that He's given you truth but you haven't responded in obedience? Have you been frustrated because the Bible doesn't seem to make sense to you? And when you pray, is it as though your prayers hit the ceiling of your room and bounce back? Have you felt as though God has abandoned you?

If so, perhaps you need to go back to the last thing you can remember that He told you, and act on it. Was it something in your pastor's message? In a daily devotion? Counsel from a godly friend?

First Peter 1:22 reminds us, "You have purified your souls in obeying the truth through the Spirit" (NKJV). In prayer, confess your sin of disobedience—whether or not it was willful. Follow your prayer of confession with intentional obedience. Then, by faith, ask God to break His silence in your life.

A SPIRITUALLY RICH DIET

These all look to you to give them their food at the proper
time. When you give it to them, they gather it up; when
you open your hand, they are satisfied with good things.
Psalm 104:27–28

God's Word describes the characteristics of Christ that are to be revealed in our lives as spiritual fruit: "love, joy, peace, patience, kindness, goodness, faithfulness, gentleness and self-control" (Galatians 5:22–23). All these characteristics of the fruit of the Spirit ought to be present in our homes.

So what kind of fruit are your children "eating" within your home? Does their diet consist of nagging, complaining, anger, bickering, gossip, selfishness, rudeness? Or are they consistently nourished as they learn to be loving when someone is not lovable, to have joy when life isn't fun, to have peace in the middle of pressure, to be kind when treated roughly?

Our homes should be places of rich moral and spiritual feeding for our children. What are you doing to provide a spiritually rich diet? Make your children hungry for good fruit ... by your example.

Take Time to Thank God

My soul glorifies the Lord and my spirit rejoices
in God my Savior, for he has been mindful of
the humble state of his servant. From now on all
generations will call me blessed, for the Mighty One
has done great things for me—holy is his name.

Luke 1:46–49

The concept of thanksgiving seemed to escape the early Israelites. They had been delivered from bondage in Egypt by God's supernatural power, yet within days, they had apparently forgotten. They began blaming God for delivering them from Egypt so they could die in the desert.

Then God again exerted His mighty power and divided the Red Sea so they could go across safely. And when they became hungry and began to whine again, God sent them fresh manna every morning!

What has God done for you recently for which you have yet to thank Him? Psalm 42:4 says, "These things I remember as I pour out my soul ... with shouts of joy and thanksgiving." What do *you* remember?

This Thanksgiving season, make a list of things you are truly thankful for. Then thank God for them.

JESUS IN YOU

*"And I will ask the Father, and he will give you
another Counselor to be with you forever."*
John 14:16

Whatever your circumstance, you have the Holy Spirit as your Counselor. Following supper the night before Jesus was to be crucified, He unburdened His heart to His disciples. He knew He would soon be leaving them when He went back to His Father in heaven after the resurrection. His disciples would be like orphans.

Although the disciples didn't grasp the magnitude of the cross and resurrection, they began to realize Jesus was going to leave them. And they must have begun to wonder. Without Jesus, how could they ever meet their own needs, much less the needs of so many others? Jesus knew their fears. He said to them, "It is for your good that I am going away. Unless I go away, the Counselor will not come to you; but if I go, I will send him to you" (John 16:7). Jesus assured them He would remain with them, not physically, but in the person of the Holy Spirit.

Jesus is always accessible, always attentive. Because the Holy Spirit is Jesus in you!

FOLLOW HIS DIRECTIONS

Your word is a lamp to my feet and a light for my path.
Psalm 119:105

God never intended you to be broken. He has specific directions for your life, and if you live according to those directions, life works and you experience life the way it was meant to be lived.

If we ignore or reject His directions, we do so to our own detriment, and we experience much less than He intended. As the psalmist wrote, "Blessed are those who keep His testimonies, who seek Him with the whole heart" (Psalm 119:2 NKJV).

God's Word is like the markings on a highway. If we and other drivers drove within the proper lines and lanes, we are more likely to travel safely to our destination. If we go outside the lines, we do so at our own peril.

God did not just create you and me and plop us down here and say, "Happy birthday. Now guess your way through life." He has given us roadway markings, directions that help to keep us safe on our journey through life.

Open your Bible and follow His directions!

LIVING HEART HEALTHY

Above all else, guard your heart, for it is the wellspring of life.
Proverbs 4:23

Some time back, one of my children had some issues with her heart that landed her in the hospital emergency room. As a result, I did a little research on the Internet and discovered that physical heart attacks usually occur when a clot blocks the flow of blood through a coronary artery, damaging or destroying part of the heart muscle. Heart attacks can be fatal because people often don't take the symptoms seriously. They confuse them with a minor illness like indigestion and thus delay going to the hospital. So recognizing the symptoms becomes critical.

My daughter's issues have been addressed, but her rather frightening episode made me think of spiritual heart attacks. While they may not be fatal to our eternal life, they can cause us to lose heart so that we are rendered ineffective in service. Instead of experiencing victory and joy, we plunge into defeat and despair, trudging our way through the Christian life as though walking through heavy mud.

Don't live with a spiritually damaged heart. Take it to Jesus. Ask Him to reveal the "clots" of sin blocking the flow of His Spirit within; confess them, and ask Him to cleanse you so that you can say, "God is the strength of my heart and my portion forever" (Psalm 73:26).

Genuine "Thanksliving"

Enter his gates with thanksgiving and his courts with
praise; give thanks to him and praise his name. For
the LORD is good and his love endures forever; his
faithfulness continues through all generations.
Psalm 100:4–5

Thanksgiving is my favorite holiday. I enjoy the *feast*: the turkey with dressing and gravy, corn pudding, sweet potato casserole. My mouth is watering just thinking about it.

But the highlight of the day is gathering around the dining room table and sharing what we're most thankful for. Paul said in Colossians 3:16–17 to "let the word of Christ dwell in you richly as you teach and admonish one another with all wisdom, and as you sing psalms, hymns and spiritual songs with gratitude in your hearts to God. And whatever you do, whether in word or deed, do it all in the name of the Lord Jesus, giving thanks to God the Father through him."

But as much as I enjoy our family's Thanksgiving Day tradition, I know that our gratitude to God isn't meant to be measured out once a year around a dining room table. It's to be genuine "thanks*living*." Tell God what you are thankful for today and every day.

OUR "ABBA" FATHER

*How great is the love the Father has lavished on
us, that we should be called children of God!*
1 John 3:1

D o you long to have a closer relationship with God, but you don't feel worthy? Are you convinced you're a nobody and therefore would never be accepted, much less welcomed, into God's presence?

The truth is, it's through faith in Jesus that we have eternal life; that faith is not just a ticket to heaven but also to a personal, intimate relationship with our heavenly Father.

The apostle Paul said, "You received the Spirit of sonship. And by him we cry, 'Abba, Father'" (Romans 8:15). When we enter God's presence, we're as accepted by God as Jesus is, because God counts us as His own dear children. Jesus invites us to come into His Father's presence through prayer, to crawl up into His lap by faith, to put our heads on His shoulder and feel His loving arms of protection around us.

God is your Abba Daddy. Pour out your heart to Him!

MORE BLESSING

"If you, then, though you are evil, know how to give good
gifts to your children, how much more will your Father
in heaven give good gifts to those who ask him!"
Matthew 7:11

How would you describe a truly blessed life? I expect that good health, sufficient wealth, and emotional happiness would be on your list. But those things are not necessarily characteristic of a truly blessed life.

The blessing God wants to pour out on us isn't attainable by reciting prayers as though you're rubbing a magic lamp, waiting for a divine genie to pop out and grant your request. The blessing God wants to give you and me can be summed up in one word—*Jesus*!

"Honor and majesty You have placed upon him. For ... You have made him exceedingly glad with Your presence" (Psalm 21:5–6 NKJV). If you want more blessing, what you're really asking for is more of Jesus! Just ask!

December

The problem of getting great things from God
is being able to hold on for the last half hour.

Mrs. Charles E. Cowman, *Streams in the Desert* (March 5)

ONLY TRUST HIM

Then Jesus said, "Did I not tell you that if you
believed, you would see the glory of God?"
John 11:40

Are you wondering why God has delayed answering your prayer? And have you reacted to the delay by trying to help Him out, speed things up? Have you turned to a lawyer, a counselor, a friend, a neighbor? Have you resorted to threats or bargaining or manipulation until you're totally exhausted? Are you at the absolute end of your rope?

One reason God may be delaying His answer to your prayer and postponing His intervention in your situation is to bring you to the end of your own resources. Proverbs 3:5 says, "Trust in the LORD with all your heart and lean not on your own understanding." Sometimes God waits in order to allow us time to exhaust every other avenue of help until we finally realize without any doubt or reservation that we're totally helpless without Him.

Trust Him. Only trust Him ... with all your heart.

FINDING PURPOSE

Now it is God who has made us for this very purpose and has
given us the Spirit as a deposit, guaranteeing what is to come.
2 Corinthians 5:5

Is there something missing in your life? An aching loneliness, a yearning
deep inside yourself for *something*? You were created with a God-shaped
hole in your heart, a capacity to know God in a personal, permanent, love
relationship.

Colossians 1:16 says, "All things were created by him and for him." And
that means you and me. God created us for a purpose, and His purpose for
your life and mine is not primarily to make us good or successful or happy
or wealthy or prosperous or problem-free. Our primary purpose is to enjoy
Him and to know Him so fully and intimately that we reflect Him in all we
are and say and do, so we can bring glory to the One who created us.

Don't miss out on your life's purpose. Discover who you were truly
meant to be. Fill the emptiness inside by establishing a love relationship
with God!

GOD IS ACTIVE IN THE DARK

And there were shepherds living out in the fields nearby,
keeping watch over their flocks at night. An angel
of the Lord appeared to them, and the glory of the
Lord shone around them, and they were terrified.
Luke 2:8–9

When she was very young, one of my granddaughters became afraid of the dark. To fall asleep she needed a night-light in her room.

I wonder if you, like my granddaughter, are also afraid of the dark. Not the dark of night but the dark times in life, when pressures, problems, pain, and even persecution envelop us in a fog of confusion or depression … those spiritually dark times when God seems far away.

Please know that from the very beginning, God has been active in the dark. At the earliest dawn of creation, the Bible says, "Now the earth was formless and empty, darkness was over the surface of the deep, and the Spirit of God was hovering" (Genesis 1:2).

If you are presently living in the darkness … of a humanly hopeless situation … of death or disease or divorce … of fear or failure or frustration … of doubt or danger … of confusion or depression … be assured that God is with you. He will change things, and He has a Word for you. God is active in the dark. Just ask the shepherds …

You're Not Alone

"Never will I leave you; never will I forsake you."
Hebrews 13:5

When have you felt lonely? Has it been even when you're in a crowd? Maybe when you're alone, without companionship? In our over-populated world, with people living in crowded cities, shopping in crowded malls, driving on crowded streets, working in crowded offices ... many people are desperately lonely.

The dictionary defines *loneliness* as "being without companionship; a feeling of desolation; depressed at being alone." Does your loneliness come from the fact that you feel unknown? Or misunderstood? Or ignored? Then you need Jesus. You need more of His nearness in your loneliness.

Jesus promised, "I will not leave you as orphans; I will come to you" (John 14:18). When you receive Jesus by faith, He comes to you in the person of His Holy Spirit, never to leave you.

And if His Spirit lives in you, you may feel lonely, but you are not alone.

WE HAVE THE ANSWER!

So do not throw away your confidence; it will be richly
rewarded. You need to persevere so that when you have
done the will of God, you will receive what he has promised.
Hebrews 10:35–36

We're bombarded with bad news. Children are abducted; storms devastate lives; people kill strangers and loved ones; people we've looked up to fail. The list goes on—and sometimes seems endless.

What bad news holds you captive? What fear hinders you from freely living for Christ? In a world of despair and increasing hopelessness, it's important that you and I do not lose our focus.

Romans 1:16 says, "I am not ashamed of the gospel, because it is the power of God for the salvation of everyone who believes." Our focus isn't on the despair, the misery and hate, or on our problems or disasters. Our focus is on Jesus and the forgiveness, freedom, and favor He offers.

People are looking for answers, for something that makes sense of the senseless and gives hope to the hopeless. You and I have the answer: it's Jesus! This is not the time to lose confidence. Proclaim the good news of the gospel!

Unanswered Prayer

By faith Abraham, even though he was past age—and Sarah
herself was barren—was enabled to become a father because
he considered him faithful who had made the promise.
Hebrews 11:11

Do you have an unanswered prayer? Not just a small request but a major, heartbreaking, soul-wrenching prayer that God has not answered? I do.

And as you have wrestled with it, have you asked, "Does God really love me?" or, "Has He heard me?" or, "Is He unable to answer?" or, "Have I done something to displease Him?"

Have you been confronted with the temptation to turn away from Him, to stop praying because He doesn't seem to be answering anyway? The apostle Paul struggled with his "thorn in my flesh" and wrote, "Three times I pleaded with the Lord to take it away from me. But he said to me, 'My grace is sufficient for you, for my power is made perfect in weakness'" (2 Corinthians 12:8–9).

Keep praying. And keep trusting. Trust Him when you don't understand and nothing makes sense. Trust Him!

DON'T PLAY IT SAFE

Now faith is being sure of what we hope for
and certain of what we do not see.
Hebrews 11:1

In what ways are you playing it safe? God reminds us that He has not given us a "spirit of timidity, but a spirit of power, of love and of self-discipline" (2 Timothy 1:7). Being overly cautious in the spiritual realm can paralyze our faith. Or, at the least, it can cause us to procrastinate until obedience becomes a burden and walking by faith slows to a crawl.

Living a life of faith requires taking risks when we can't physically see what lies ahead, or hear what God is saying, or know what He is thinking, or feel what He is doing. We have to be willing to take the risk of failure—of possibly being mistaken or of making fools of ourselves. We have to trust His Word, and His Word alone.

Don't play it safe and miss out on receiving everything God wants to give you. It's more than worth it! The truth is, faith is not a risk at all. It is a certainty because God is as good as His Word.

Step Out in Faith

But he took her by the hand and said, "My child, get up!"
Luke 8:54

I'm often asked, "How can I know the major decision I'm making is God's will?" Sometimes, when our circumstances just don't seem to line up, God may be requiring a step of faith. Think of it this way: when the children of Israel crossed the Jordan River, they had to get their feet wet before the waters rolled back.

Ask God to confirm your decision with Scripture. Seek the counsel of godly people. And know that if God closes the door, you can't force it open. Don't manipulate circumstances to make your decision work.

As you walk by faith, you will increasingly have a deep inner confidence that your decision is of God. Psalm 25:9 says, "He guides the humble in what is right and teaches them his way."

If you want to do what's right and walk in God's way, not your own, He will guide you. But to be guided, you must get up and take the first step.

It's Time to Get Serious

"Who then is the faithful and wise servant, whom the master
has put in charge of the servants in his household to give
them their food at the proper time? It will be good for that
servant whose master finds him doing so when he returns."

Matthew 24:45–46

The words of Jesus continuously motivate me: "As long as it is day, we must do the work of him who sent me. Night is coming, when no one can work" (John 9:4). Time is running out. Night *is* coming. It's time to get serious: the time to serve God is *now*!

I can almost hear John's voice raised in the chorus of Revelation: "Worthy is the Lamb, who was slain" (5:12). Can you sing it now, not just by the words you say, but by the life you live and the serious service you give? God doesn't want casual Christians in His service.

In the Old Testament, He whittled down Gideon's army from thirty-two thousand men to three hundred by cutting out those who did not take service to Him more seriously than anything else. In God's army today, would you make the cut? It's time to get serious!

ARE YOU READY?

Early in the morning Joshua and all the Israelites
set out from Shittim and went to the Jordan.
Joshua 3:1

Are you ready to step out for God? Maybe He's challenging you to walk across the street and share the gospel with a neighbor. Or to live out your faith in Christ at your workplace.

An incredibly rich dimension of knowing God is reserved for those who step out of their comfort zones and walk by faith. Is God challenging *you*?

The Israelites wandered for forty years, just going in circles and never really getting anywhere. Then God instructed them, under Joshua's leadership, to step out of where they'd been and into all that He wanted to give them. It was a challenge that became very personal to Joshua. God told him, "Be strong and courageous, because you will lead these people to inherit the land I swore to their forefathers to give them" (Joshua 1:6).

It's time for you to leave the wilderness ... to enter into the fullness of blessing God has for you. But you have to take the first step.

YOUR WAKE-UP CALL

Wake up! Strengthen what remains and is about to die.
Revelation 3:2

Is your heart broken for those who are stepping into eternity, lost forever? Are you grieved for the church that has a "form of godliness" but denies God's power (2 Timothy 3:5)? Then this is your wake-up call—your spiritual wake-up call!

The daily routine of responsibilities, the never-ending challenge of deadlines, the persistent pressure of problems, and the hectic pace of life tend to preoccupy our thoughts and time. If we're not careful, we may miss something vitally important that God has for us. Something He may want us to see or do.

Isaiah overheard "the voice of the Lord saying, 'Whom shall I send? And who will go for us?'" And Isaiah volunteered, "Here am I. Send me!" (Isaiah 6:8). Isaiah responded to God, committed his life to serving Him, and became the greatest of the Old Testament prophets.

Open *your* eyes! It's time to wake up!

LISTENING FOR HIS VOICE

In the first year of his reign, I, Daniel, understood from the
Scriptures, according to the word of the LORD given to Jeremiah
the prophet, that the desolation of Jerusalem would last seventy
years. So I turned to the Lord God and pleaded with him in
prayer and petition, in fasting, and in sackcloth and ashes.

Daniel 9:2–3

When you read your Bible, are you listening for God's voice to speak to you through it? Communication requires both talking and listening. And our relationship with God is no exception to that basic rule.

We communicate with Him by talking to Him in prayer and by listening to Him as we read our Bible. His Word gives encouragement in despair, comfort in isolation, light in darkness, joy in tears, purpose in struggle, wisdom in decisions. His Word "is a lamp to my feet and a light for my path" (Psalm 119:105).

Through God's Word, we know Him, and He gives acceptance in rejection, love in loneliness, grace in failures, hope in grief. How can we exist without Him? And how could we ever begin to know Him without His Word?

Listen for the voice of God to speak to you ... with your eyes on the pages of your Bible.

A LIFE SURVEY

*. . . being confident of this, that he who began a good work in
you will carry it on to completion until the day of Christ Jesus.*
Philippians 1:6

Sometime back, my husband and I decided to remodel our then fifty-five-year-old kitchen. Because of the increasingly busy pace of my life, I had let things go until there was no practical remedy except to tear everything out and start over. I had to brace myself for the sound and sight of the old being smashed, torn out, and discarded. Suddenly I was focused on executing the plan that had been prayerfully and painstakingly laid out, knowing I would need perseverance to see the project through to completion.

In some ways, my life is like that kitchen. I have decided to survey the condition of my life to make sure I'm not letting things go until drastic change is required. While studying the book of Hebrews, I was challenged to research the lives of others as role models for my own life—to tear out and repent of sin that impedes the effectiveness of my Christian life and to refocus on the goal of a life lived for God's glory and honor, a life that brings Him pleasure as it reflects His own Son.

Isn't it time you surveyed the condition of *your* life? Surrender it completely to the Master Builder, giving Him full authority to seeing your transformation through to completion.

You're Never Alone

Be strong and courageous. Do not be afraid or terrified
because of them, for the Lord your God goes with
you; he will never leave you nor forsake you.

Deuteronomy 31:6

If you're lonely, don't withdraw into an uninvolved, inactive life. It only intensifies the loneliness. Welcome God into your life to share your loneliness while you walk with Him and work for Him.

Two thousand years ago, a solitary figure stood out in history. The Bible says the sin of all mankind was placed on Him as He walked to the place of sacrifice, carrying His own means of execution. He was betrayed by one of His best friends and denied by another. Not one person stood with Him. Not the blind man to whom He'd given sight. Or the leper He'd cleansed.

He was crucified on a Roman cross, alone.

Jesus understands loneliness. He endured it for you. So know that regardless of your circumstances, you need never be alone. Jesus said, "Surely I am with you always, to the very end of the age" (Matthew 28:20).

HE IS LOVE

"I am the Alpha and the Omega," says the Lord God, "who
is, and who was, and who is to come, the Almighty."

Revelation 1:8

What comfort to remember that Jesus promised, "I will never leave you nor forsake you" (Hebrews 13:5 NKJV). What comfort! What security! What encouragement! You and I can be where Jesus is now and for all eternity because He lives in us—and He has promised He always will.

Others may leave us through death or abandonment. A spouse may leave us through divorce. A disease may threaten to rob us of someone we love. But God will never leave us. When the fire of adversity increases in intensity, we have God's presence. When we are overwhelmed by burdens or depression, by loneliness or betrayal, we have His presence.

There is not one place in the entire universe, visible or invisible, where Jesus is not! Including right there where you are. Right now.

THE ALL-MIGHTY

Jesus Christ is the same yesterday and today and forever.

Hebrews 13:8

No one—no thing—is mightier than Jesus!

He is God Almighty.

And He always has been, always is, always will be.

He is the everlasting Father, eternally the same yesterday, today, and forever.

There's no age in history or in the future where He will not be present—in every generation—in every culture—in every nation. Be assured He is fully present with you even as you read these words. He's with those you love.

Jesus Christ is fully in charge.

He is the Lord God.

He makes no mistakes.

He never second-guesses Himself.

You will never face anything He cannot handle. Put your faith in the One who is Almighty.

A Root of Bitterness

See to it that no one misses the grace of God and that no
bitter root grows up to cause trouble and defile many.
Hebrews 12:15

Some of the most miserable people are those who have unconfessed sin and rebellion in their hearts against God. Cain is the perfect example. He had not only been created *by* God; he had been created *for* God. But Genesis 4:16 says, "Cain went out from the LORD's presence and lived in the land of Nod, east of Eden."

Either the sin in the presence of a holy, *righteous* God must be confessed and cleansed, or the sinner must leave God's presence. What a tragedy. Cain's life illustrates the hard lesson. If you refuse to turn to God in repentance, guilt will drive you away from Him. Bitterness-rooted resentment and rebellion can impact a family for generations to follow. Cain's descendants were notorious for their wickedness.

Don't leave the presence of God. Confess your sin now. Your descendants will be blessed.

MY PEACE

"Peace I leave with you; my peace I give you. I
do not give to you as the world gives. Do not let
your hearts be troubled and do not be afraid."

John 14:27

Do you lack peace? Are you afraid? What gives you panic attacks? Why does your stomach turn over and your face drain of color and your heart race at just the thought of whatever it is? The psalmist said, "Great peace have they who love your law" (Psalm 119:165). God will give you and me promises that bring peace in the midst of our panic, but we must tune our hearts to listen to His voice.

When David was running for his life from King Saul, he found himself in great danger in every situation. The temptation to worry must have been overwhelming. But he wrote, "In God, whose word I praise, in God I trust; I will not be afraid" (Psalm 56:4).

Stop worrying! Start reading His Word. Trust in Him. Peace will come!

FULLY COMMITTED

"Go up and down the streets of Jerusalem, look
around and consider, search through her squares.
If you can find but one person who deals honestly
and seeks the truth, I will forgive this city."
Jeremiah 5:1

Are you willing to be one who lives out the truth? That one person who confesses publicly as well as privately, "Jesus is Lord"? That one person who has the courage and boldness to stand for godly convictions in the midst of the moral compromise that abounds? Can you be that one person?

Second Chronicles 16:9 says, "For the eyes of the LORD range throughout the earth to strengthen those whose hearts are fully committed to him." What is keeping *you* from being fully committed? Is it the opinions of others? Or the demands of your business? Perhaps some habit or sin you are enjoying for the moment? Could it be that your lack of spiritual strength and your weak faith are directly related to your halfhearted commitment?

Two thousand years ago, God fully committed Himself to you when He sent Jesus. This Christmas, would you fully commit yourself to Him? Be the one person He is looking for.

LOOK AT THE STAR

*They went on their way, and the star they had
seen in the east went ahead of them until it
stopped over the place where the child was. When
they saw the star, they were overjoyed.*
Matthew 2:9–10

Our senses are bombarded 24/7 by sounds and sights, especially during the Christmas season. Marketing companies compete, all trying to get our attention. They spend millions for what they're selling and promoting, not to mention holiday parties, church programs, and school plays.

I wonder what I would have used to get the world to look at a tiny baby in a manger. How would I have drawn attention to an obscure stable behind some inn in an obscure Judean town?

When God wanted to get the attention of the nations of the world, He used a star. When the Magi came from the east to Jerusalem, they asked, "Where is the one who has been born king of the Jews? We saw his star in the east and have come to worship him" (Matthew 2:2).

This Christmas, be His star! Ask God to use you to draw the attention of others to the Baby in the manger.

THE ONLY WAY

This is how God showed his love among us: He sent his one
and only Son into the world that we might live through him.

1 John 4:9

Do you think there is more than one way to God? Have you bought into popular opinion that seems to think you can pick and choose your religion—even make one up to suit yourself?

If this is the way you're thinking, heed the words in 1 Timothy 2:5: "There is one God and one mediator between God and men, the man Christ Jesus."

The politically correct say Jesus was a good man, a well-meaning prophet, even a revolutionary! But the Bible says He is the only Mediator between God and man: "There is no other name under heaven given to men by which we must be saved" (Acts 4:12).

Jesus Himself said, "I am the way and the truth and the life. No one comes to the Father except through me" (John 14:6). Don't allow political correctness to rob you of a relationship with the one true God. This Christmas season, give God a gift He wants. Tell someone how to come to Him ... through Jesus.

GOD IS WITH YOU

"The virgin will be with child and will give birth to a son, and
they will call him Immanuel"—which means, "God with us."
Matthew 1:23

God doesn't always protect you from suffering or answer your prayers the way you ask Him to. But He does promise in His Word that He will be present with you in life.

Isn't that one of the supreme revelations of Christmas? That God came down to be with us in our joy, in our sorrow, in our struggles, in our hopes, in our dreams. He came down to be with us in our families and our friendships. God is with us!

Philippians 2:6–7 says that Jesus, "being in very nature God,... made himself nothing, taking the very nature of a servant, being made in human likeness."

God draws near to those who are suffering. He is with you—now!

IN THE MOOD

We give thanks to you, Lord God Almighty, the
One who is and who was, because you have taken
your great power and have begun to reign.
Revelation 11:17

There are moments when I'm just not in the mood for Christmas! So how are we to catch the real Christmas spirit if we're not "in the mood"? The house may be decorated. You may attend parties, go caroling, buy gifts, cook, bake. But is it all just a holiday hassle to you?

Several years ago, I got burned out at Christmas. Then I asked Jesus, as the King, what He would like for His birthday. That totally transformed my attitude.

Now, each year as I ask Jesus again, He whispers something into my heart that I can do for Him. It's always something that's sacrificial in nature. But more than any other single factor, it's what adds sparkle to my Christmas.

The wise men "opened their treasures and presented [Jesus] with gifts" (Matthew 2:11). What gift will you present the King this year for His birthday?

CELEBRATE JESUS

> For to us a child is born, to us a son is given, and
> the government will be on his shoulders. And
> he will be called Wonderful Counselor, Mighty
> God, Everlasting Father, Prince of Peace.
> *Isaiah 9:6*

Our culture has become so secularized there are many people who don't know who Jesus truly is. In fact, some people even see Jesus as offensive and controversial. Consider celebrating Christmas by maintaining your genuine worship of Christ.

But who is Jesus to you? And how, in the midst of all the busyness, loneliness, religiousness, and happiness that swirls throughout the holidays, will you celebrate the real meaning of Christmas this year?

John 1:4 says, "In [Jesus] was life, and that life was the light of men." The apostle John saw Jesus and said, "Look, the Lamb of God, who takes away the sin of the world!" (John 1:29).

Who is Jesus? He is God wrapped in swaddling clothes, lying in a manger. He is the Creator who became your Savior. Celebrate *Him.* He's the reason for the season. Celebrate Jesus!

Born of the Spirit

> "Flesh gives birth to flesh, but the Spirit gives birth to spirit."
> *John 3:6*

When the angel Gabriel appeared to Mary, he gave her a startling announcement: "The Holy Spirit will come upon you, and the power of the Most High will overshadow you. So the holy one to be born will be called the Son of God" (Luke 1:35).

What happened to Mary physically happens to you and me spiritually. When you and I place our faith in Jesus Christ and invite Him to come live within us, the Holy Spirit overshadows us and the spiritual life of Jesus is born within us. Jesus told Nicodemus, one of the religious leaders of his time, "You must be born again" (John 3:7).

The hope that was born that night in Bethlehem continues to radiate down through the years. You can start over. You can become a new person. You can be born again. You *must* be born again!

GIVE UP YOUR RIGHTS

Being in very nature God, [Jesus] did not consider
equality with God something to be grasped.... and being
found in appearance as a man, he humbled himself and
became obedient to death—even death on a cross!
Philippians 2:6, 8

Do you always have to be right? Sometimes the solution to a problem is just to give up and let go of your right to be right. To give up your right to special attention, your right to go first, your right to a certain place, a certain privilege. Just give it up.

Don't let pride or selfishness keep you from solving the problem and restoring peace in your home or office or church. Paul urged the early church members to set aside their own selfishness, desires, and rights when he commanded, "Make every effort to keep the unity of the Spirit through the bond of peace" (Ephesians 4:3).

While the world exhorts you and me to insist on our rights, Bethlehem shows us that's not God's way. Who's watching you and the way you handle your problems and disputes? Demonstrate to a watching world how God's children solve conflicts! Humble yourself. Keep the unity by giving up your rights.

GETTING WHAT YOU WANT

Do not be deceived: God cannot be
mocked. A man reaps what he sows.
Galatians 6:7

What are you insisting on getting, having, owning, being, doing, possessing? Watch out! If you insist on selfishly getting what you want, you just may get it—and wind up with a lot less than what God wants to give you.

Consider the story of Lot, who selfishly chose for himself the whole plain of Jordan, pitched his tents near Sodom, and then moved in to a very wicked world—a world without any fear of God. The long-term consequences for Lot were disastrous. He's referred to in 2 Peter 2:7–8 as one who "was distressed by the filthy lives of lawless men (for that *righteous* man, living among them day after day, was tormented in his *righteous* soul by the lawless deeds he saw and heard)" (italics mine). Lot was miserable—but he stayed in Sodom.

Scripture tells us God is not mocked. Sinfulness may bring momentary pleasures and satisfaction, but it leads to misery and lasting destruction! As you reflect on the past year and look ahead to the next, stop insisting on what *you* want. Ask God to give you what *He* wants in the New Year.

TAKE GOD AT HIS WORD

"For God so loved the world that he gave his
one and only Son, that whoever believes in him
shall not perish but have eternal life."
John 3:16

Has something bad happened to you? If so, do you think it means God doesn't really know what's going on? Or worse, maybe He knows, but He's not pleased with you or He doesn't love you? Are you interpreting His love by your circumstances—instead of interpreting your circumstances by His love?

When you're tempted to question whether or not God cares, remember Christmas and the Baby of Bethlehem. Jesus said, "The Father himself loves you because you have loved me and have believed that I came from God" (John 16:27).

When tempted to doubt God's love, take a good look at the heart of God wrapped in swaddling clothes, lying in a manger. God loves you so much that He has given you Jesus.

Born of the Spirit

"The Holy Spirit will come upon you, and the power
of the Most High will overshadow you. So the holy
one to be born will be called the Son of God."

Luke 1:35

Everyone living on planet Earth has been physically born. But if we want to go to heaven, there's something more. We must also be born of the Spirit. John 3:5 says, "Unless one is born of water and the Spirit, he cannot enter the kingdom of God" (NKJV).

You and I conceive the spiritual life of the Son of God when we're "born again." When that takes place, we have the mind, the emotions, and the will that we're physically born with. But now we also have the mind, the emotions, and the will of the Son of God. It's like a spiritual implant of the life of Jesus Christ in our bodies. It's a supernatural miracle, something God does in response to our humble confession and sincere repentance of sin—and our deliberate, personal faith in Jesus Christ.

It is possible, as you look ahead to the New Year, to truly have a fresh start. A brand-new beginning. You can be born again!

LOVE JESUS MORE

Jesus replied: "Love the Lord your God with all your
heart and with all your soul and with all your mind."
Matthew 22:37

D o you love me?" *"Do* you love me?" "Do *you* love me?" When Jesus
asked Peter the question three times (see John 21:15, 16, 17; italics are
mine), what was He really searching for?

Maybe Jesus was asking, "Peter, do you love Me more than yourself? Do
you love Me more than the opinion of others? More than your own safety
and comfort? More than your reputation? More than the memories of sin
and failure? More than your career?"

Jesus was reaching into Peter's heart and putting His finger on Peter's
core. Peter had just denied Jesus. Now Jesus was challenging Peter to love
Him more—and then to express his love through serving Him.

What about you? Is your motivation to serve Jesus an attempt to cover
up guilty feelings? Or to earn forgiveness? Or to avoid criticism? Are you
trying to prove something, to gain approval or recognition? Or is your primary motivation because you sincerely love Jesus more than anything?

Resolve this next year to love Jesus more than anything. Then let your
heart overflow in service.

Finishing the Race

*I pray that out of his glorious riches he may strengthen
you with power through his Spirit in your inner being.*
Ephesians 3:16

As the runners flew around the track in the 1992 Summer Olympics, one man pulled up on the backstretch and limped to a stop. He'd pulled a hamstring. As the crowd stood, a man ran out of the stands to the young athlete. The microphones picked up the runner's words: "Dad, you've got to help me across the finish line. I've trained all my life for this race." The father put his arm around his son, and together they limped across the finish line—to a standing ovation.

In this race of life, when you think you can't go one more step, the Holy Spirit will wrap His everlasting arms around you and walk with you to the finish! Jesus promised, "I will ask the Father, and he will give you another Counselor to be with you forever" (John 14:16).

When our race here on earth ends, the Holy Spirit will help us cross the finish line—as the applause of heaven rings in our ears!

Scripture Index

4:43, June 14
6:12, September 20
6:37, March 30
8:54, December 8
9:12–13, October 28
9:13, March 15
9:16–17, October 28
11:1–2, February 1
11:13, August 3
11:34, September 30
14:33, September 18
15:20, November 20
18:16, June 12, August 17
19:40, January 16
22:42, May 7
23:34, March 30, May 27
23:35, September 14
24:27, July 6
24:28–29, October 27
24:45, July 12

JOHN

1:1, November 17
1:1–2, August 26
1:3, August 27, November 12
1:4, December 24
1:5, August 28, November 7
1:9, August 28, November 17
1:12, February 1, March 20, November 6
1:12–13, March 20
1:16, February 7
1:16–17, October 23
1:17, August 31
1:18, September 29
1:29, December 24
2:1–2, September 2
2:3, April 9
2:4, April 9
2:5, April 9
3:3, September 4
3:5, December 29
3:6, December 25
3:7, February 9, February 16, September 4,

December 25
3:8, September 4
3:16, March 28, April 11, September 5, December 28
3:19, November 7
3:29, February 27
3:36, September 4
4:4, May 19
4:6, May 19
4:10, September 7
4:13, June 26
4:14, June 26
4:23, September 6
4:24, September 6
4:29, September 25
5:6–7, March 26
6:3, January 2
6:7, August 1
6:8–9, August 1
6:12, June 11
6:35, September 17
6:44, February 4
7:38, September 7
8:12, March 17, July 27, August 28
8:36, March 27, July 4
9:1–3, May 2
9:3, May 2, October 25
9:4, May 26, December 9
10:3–4, March 14, May 20
10:4, January 23
10:10, April 16, October 24
10:11, April 10
10:14, January 12
10:14–15, April 16
10:30, August 26
11:3, August 30
11:21, May 29, August 10
11:23, May 29
11:25–26, May 29
11:33, April 13, September 26
11:35, January 13
11:40, November 2, December 1
12:3, August 2
12:5, January 14
12:7, January 14

2 PETER
1:3, July 25, August 12
2:7–8, December 27

1 JOHN
1:1, January 16, September 3
1:3–4, April 5, November 8
1:5, March 17, September 29
1:7, March 17
1:9, February 24, August 11, September 12, September 13, October 20
2:1–2, February 25
2:5, April 15
2:5–6, May 30
3:1, July 15, November 29
3:2, November 11
3:16, October 29
3:18–19, June 8
4:4, July 8
4:7, April 20
4:8, July 15
4:9, December 21
4:13–14, July 3
4:16, January 24, April 18, July 15
4:19, February 4
5:14, August 30
5:14–15, November 5

2 JOHN
1:3, February 16

JUDE
24, September 27

REVELATION
1:8, December 15
1:12, May 12
1:17, January 10
2:4–5, February 14
2:10, June 10
3:1, April 6
3:2, December 11
3:8, March 2, March 22, October 2
3:12, October 2
5:12, April 12, July 16, December 9
11:17, December 23
19:7–8, March 31
19:15, January 29
21:1, February 22
21:1–2, August 14
21:2, July 1
21:3, June 29, August 14
21:4, June 29, August 15
21:5, February 22
21:7, August 21
21:14, June 30
21:27, February 27
22:1, January 28
22:3–4, August 15
22:17, January 28, March 24

ABOUT THE AUTHOR

 A nne Graham Lotz is a bestselling and award-winning author of thirteen books, including *The Daniel Prayer.* She is the president of AnGeL Ministries, Raleigh, North Carolina. Called "the best preacher in the family" by her father, Billy Graham, Anne speaks around the globe with the wisdom and authority of years spent studying God's Word. The *New York Times* named Anne one of the five most influential evangelists of her generation.

After reading this book, if you need additional resources to help you embrace the God-filled life, please contact Anne Graham Lotz through one of the following means:

AnGeL Ministries
5115 Hollyridge Drive
Raleigh, North Carolina 27612
919.787.6606
www.AnneGrahamLotz.org